21世纪全国高职高专土建立体化系列规划教材

建筑工程专业英语

主　编　韩　薇　张华明
副主编　张军历　张益荣

内 容 简 介

本书是高等职业技术院校建筑工程相关专业的专业英语教材。本书的任务是使学生能够在学习了普通英语和建筑工程专业课的基础上，培养学生借助工具书阅读和翻译建筑工程专业英语文章的能力，掌握必备的建筑工程专业英语词汇及术语，为今后在学习和工作中获取专业信息、掌握学科发展动态、参加国际性学术交流等奠定良好的基础。

本书以培养学生的专业英语阅读能力为主要目标，共 10 个单元，每个单元都有一个主题，内容涉及土木工程师、建筑工程概论、建筑构造、建筑材料、施工测量、建筑设计、建筑结构、建筑设备、建筑施工管理和建筑节能。

本书可供高职高专院校建筑工程相关专业的学生使用，也可作为具备一定英语基础的工程技术人员及自学者的参考书。

图书在版编目(CIP)数据

建筑工程专业英语/韩薇，张华明主编．—北京：北京大学出版社，2012.1
（21 世纪全国高职高专土建立体化系列规划教材）
ISBN 978-7-301-20003-2

Ⅰ.①建… Ⅱ.①韩…②张… Ⅲ.①建筑工程—英语—高等职业教育—教材 Ⅳ.①H31

中国版本图书馆 CIP 数据核字(2011)第 277652 号

书　　　名：	建筑工程专业英语
著作责任者：	韩　薇　张华明　主编
策 划 编 辑：	赖　青　李　辉
责 任 编 辑：	姜晓楠
标 准 书 号：	ISBN 978-7-301-20003-2/TU·0209
出　 版　 者：	北京大学出版社
地　　　址：	北京市海淀区成府路 205 号　　100871
网　　　址：	http://www.pup.cn　　http://www.pup6.cn
电　　　话：	邮购部 62752015　　发行部 62750672　　编辑部 62750667　　出版部 62754962
电 子 邮 箱：	pup_6@163.com
印　 刷　 者：	三河市博文印刷有限公司
发　 行　 者：	北京大学出版社
经　 销　 者：	新华书店
	787 毫米×1092 毫米　16 开本　12 印张　272 千字
	2012 年 1 月第 1 版　　2014 年 7 月第 2 次印刷
定　　　价：	24.00 元

未经许可，不得以任何方式复制或抄袭本书之部分或全部内容。
版权所有，侵权必究。　　　举报电话：010-62752024
　　　　　　　　　　　　　电子邮箱：fd@pup.pku.edu.cn

北大版·高职高专土建系列规划教材
专家编审指导委员会

主　　　任：于世玮（山西建筑职业技术学院）

副　主　任：范文昭（山西建筑职业技术学院）

委　　　员：（按姓名拼音排序）

丁　胜（湖南城建职业技术学院）

郝　俊（内蒙古建筑职业技术学院）

胡六星（湖南城建职业技术学院）

李永光（内蒙古建筑职业技术学院）

马景善（浙江同济科技职业学院）

王秀花（内蒙古建筑职业技术学院）

王云江（浙江建设职业技术学院）

危道军（湖北城建职业技术学院）

吴承霞（河南建筑职业技术学院）

吴明军（四川建筑职业技术学院）

夏万爽（邢台职业技术学院）

徐锡权（日照职业技术学院）

战启芳（石家庄铁路职业技术学院）

杨甲奇（四川交通职业技术学院）

朱吉顶（河南工业职业技术学院）

特邀顾问：何　辉（浙江建设职业技术学院）

姚谨英（四川绵阳水电学校）

北大版·高职高专土建系列规划教材
专家编审指导委员会专业分委会

建筑工程技术专业分委会

主　任：吴承霞　　吴明军
副主任：郝　俊　　徐锡权　　马景善　　战启芳
委　员：（按姓名拼音排序）
　　　　白丽红　　陈东佐　　邓庆阳　　范优铭　　李　伟
　　　　刘晓平　　鲁有柱　　马景善　　孟胜国　　石立安
　　　　王美芬　　王渊辉　　肖明和　　叶海青　　叶　腾
　　　　叶　雯　　于全发　　曾庆军　　张　敏　　张　勇
　　　　赵华玮　　郑仁贵　　钟汉华　　朱永祥

工程管理专业分委会

主　任：危道军
副主任：胡六星　　李永光　　杨甲奇
委　员：（按姓名拼音排序）
　　　　冯　钢　　冯松山　　姜新春　　赖先志　　李柏林
　　　　李洪军　　刘志麟　　林滨滨　　时　思　　斯　庆
　　　　宋　健　　孙　刚　　唐茂华　　韦盛泉　　吴孟红
　　　　辛艳红　　鄢维峰　　杨庆丰　　余景良　　赵建军
　　　　钟振宇　　周业梅

建筑设计专业分委会

主　任：丁　胜
副主任：夏万爽　　朱吉顶
委　员：（按姓名拼音排序）
　　　　戴碧锋　　宋劲军　　脱忠伟　　王　蕾
　　　　肖伦斌　　余　辉　　张　峰　　赵志文

市政工程专业分委会

主　任：王秀花
副主任：王云江
委　员：（按姓名拼音排序）
　　　　翁金贵　　胡红英　　来丽芳　　刘　江　　刘水林
　　　　刘　雨　　张晓战　　刘宗波　　杨仲元

前　　言

"建筑工程专业英语"是根据大学英语教学大纲的要求设置的基础英语课程的后续课程。开设专业英语课程的目的是通过该课程的学习，培养学生能够借助工具书阅读和翻译土建类专业英语文章的能力，掌握各课所描述的相关专业知识，熟悉科技论文写作的基本知识，为扩大专业词汇量以及今后学习工作中获取专业信息、掌握学科发展动态、参加国际性学术交流等奠定良好的基础。

本书准确地把握了土木建筑专业相关学科之间的关系，内容丰富，同时力求精练。编者从常规的认知习惯出发，对本书内容的编排进行了全新的尝试，打破传统教材的编写模式，尽可能将理论与工程实际相联系，突出职业教育的教材特点。本书各章内容由土木建筑所包含的知识体系导入，然后展开理论描述，严谨完整，切合实际，符合课堂的教学模式，方便学生透彻地理解理论知识在工程实际中的运用。另外，内容体系的运用不局限于某一地区，而是全国适用的。

本书共10个单元，每个单元都有一个主题，内容涉及土木工程师、建筑工程概论、建筑构造、建筑材料、施工测量等。每个单元由两篇文章组成：Text 为课内阅读材料，课后给出了相应的专业词汇注解，对课文中的难点、重点进行了具体讲解，并配有针对性较强的练习，便于教师及时、有效地检查学生对课文的掌握程度；此外还有对应的参考译文便于学生自学。Reading Material 为课外阅读材料，阅读材料的选取注重趣味性和科普性。书后附有总词汇表，科技论文的写作格式及规范，科技英语的翻译以及建筑工程专业英语词汇。

本书由甘肃建筑职业技术学院韩薇、张华明担任主编，由甘肃政法学院张军历、甘肃省临夏中学张益荣担任副主编，全书由韩薇统稿。本书具体章节编写分工为：第4、第5、第7、第8单元由韩薇编写，第1、第9、第10单元由张华明编写，第2、第6单元由张军历编写，第3单元由张益荣编写。

由于编者水平有限，书中难免有不当之处，恳请广大读者批评指正。

编　者
2011年10月

目　　录

Unit 1　Civil Engineers ………………………………………………………………… 1
　　　Text：About Civil Engineers …………………………………………………… 1
　　　Reading Material：Make the Most of Your Journey ………………………… 9
Unit 2　Building Engineering …………………………………………………………… 12
　　　Text：Construction Engineering ……………………………………………… 12
　　　Reading Material：Different Types of Buildings …………………………… 19
Unit 3　Building Components ………………………………………………………… 23
　　　Text：Components of a Building ……………………………………………… 23
　　　Reading Material：Beijing Siheyuan ………………………………………… 33
Unit 4　Building Materials ……………………………………………………………… 38
　　　Text：Concrete as a Structural Material ……………………………………… 38
　　　Reading Material：Brick Manufacture and Use in Construction …………… 46
Unit 5　Construction Surveying ………………………………………………………… 51
　　　Text：What "Construction Surveying" is About ……………………………… 51
　　　Reading Material：The Purpose of the Survey ……………………………… 59
Unit 6　Building Design ………………………………………………………………… 63
　　　Text：One of the Architectural Design Values—Aesthetic Design Values … 63
　　　Reading Material：Model Types ……………………………………………… 71
Unit 7　Building Structures …………………………………………………………… 76
　　　Text：Structural Types of Building …………………………………………… 76
　　　Reading Material：Underground Construction ……………………………… 83
Unit 8　Building Facilities ……………………………………………………………… 88
　　　Text：Classification of Construction Equipment ……………………………… 88
　　　Reading Material：Choosing Construction Equipment ……………………… 98
Unit 9　Building Construction Management ………………………………………… 101
　　　Text：Construction Management ……………………………………………… 101
　　　Reading Material：The Architect as Construction Manager ……………… 108
Unit 10　Energy-saving Buildings …………………………………………………… 112
　　　　Text：Low Carbon Buildings—Target Zero Carbon Construction ……… 112
　　　　Reading Material：Green Buildings ………………………………………… 120
Vocabulary　New Words and Expressions ………………………………………… 125
附录Ⅰ　科技论文的写作格式及规范 ………………………………………………… 154
附录Ⅱ　科技英语的翻译 ……………………………………………………………… 159
附录Ⅲ　建筑工程专业英语词汇 ……………………………………………………… 167
参考文献 ………………………………………………………………………………… 180

Unit 1

Civil Engineers

Text: About Civil Engineers

Career Compasses

Get your bearings on what it takes to become a successful civil engineer.

Mathematical skills in order to make the technical calculations necessary to a projects' design (30%).

Relevant knowledge of the different factors involved in the construction of a project, and how each one affects the others (25%).

Communication skills to be able to clearly convey ideas and design concepts to the various people involved in a project (25%).

Ability to manage stress in a job field that demands strict adherence to deadlines, the ability to solve problem under pressure, and constant multi-tasking (20%).

Destination: Civil Engineers

We have come to expect a lot for our modern lives. We expect subway cars to transport us to our destination. We expect our road not to flood when it rains. We expect bridges not to collapse when we drive over them. We are able to take these expectations for granted thanks to the careful planning of a civil engineer(Fig. 1.1).

Fig. 1.1 The Goal Programming of Civil Engineers

In short, civil engineers make things work. They figure out how the infrastructures we use, and the structures we build can be designed to function effectively. Civil engineers use their knowledge of scientific and mathematic principles, and their understanding of economic and environmental factors, to plan and oversee a project's design and construction. Usually, civil engineers are hired to work on large-scale projects that will affect many people.

In addition to designing new projects, civil engineers are also hired to help upgrade existing ones. As the world's population increases, the systems we depend on—such as water supply, waste management, and transportation networks—must be adjusted. More people in the world means increased pollution and fewer natural resources to go around. It is a civil engineer's job to figure out how we can function and progress as a civilization without depleting our planet's resources, which is why job opportunities in this field are plentiful even during the times of economic crisis. In fact, employment in civil engineering is predicted to grow by 18 percent over the course of the next decade.

Although certain civil engineers(usually referred to as "site" engineers)oversee all aspects of work in one specialized discipline. There are six major civil engineering disciplines. Structural engineering focuses on how structures such as buildings, tunnels, and bridges can be designed to support themselves, and to withstand wear and tear. Construction engineering deals with overseeing all aspects of a project's construction: duties range from developing project sites to evaluating supplies to drafting employment contracts. Water resources engineering focuses on the methods of managing and collecting water as a natural resource. Environmental engineering (formerly known as sanitary engineering) focuses on pollution control, waste management, recycling systems, and the public health issues that may potentially arise from flaws in these facilities. Transportation engineering focuses on planning, constructing, and maintaining the infrastructures that get people from here to there, such as roadways, trains systems, airports, water ports, and subway systems. Geotechnical engineering focuses on how rocks, soil, terrain, and other geological components of the planet influence our infrastructures.

A civil engineer's duties on a project vary depending on the particular discipline. If you are a geotechnical or environmental engineer, a lot of your work may be done outside, researching a project site's landscape or soil alongside a surveyor. If you are a construction engineer, you might work both outside troubleshooting construction problems and inside writing plan specifications and contracts. For urban projects, part of your duties might include meeting with city administrators to discuss certain factors such as drainage codes, zoning regulations, pollution control laws, and community consensus results.

As a civil engineer in any discipline, you must be both practical and creative. You must possess practical knowledge about scientific and mathematic principles toward new design solutions. You must also have good communication skills, as the construction of large-scale projects depends upon the collaboration of many different people. You must also be good with details, deadlines, and multitasking in order to make sure that the different facets of a design plan will work together.

Unlike an architect, who usually designs a single building that will affect a limited number of people, a civil engineer designs infrastructures that can affect entire cities. Overseeing projects on such a large scale puts an immense amount of pressure on the engineer to succeed. If a project fails, you can be held at fault, and in the worst cases, you could be charged with criminal negligence. If a project runs over budget or schedule, or a design needs rethinking, you must be willing to put in extra hours to find solutions for these problems. It is up to you as a civil engineer to make sure that everyone else involved in a project's completion is not wasting his or her efforts on faulty design. Civil engineering means a lot of responsibilities, and you must be very confident in your abilities and tirelessly dedicated to your work. On average, civil engineers work a standard 40-hour week. However, their schedule is subject to change depending on certain phases of construction.

New Words and Expressions

relevant	[ˈreləvənt]	a.	有关的；切题的
collapse	[kəˈlæps]	vi.	倒坍，塌下；崩溃；突然失败
infrastructure	[ˈinfrəˌstrʌktʃə]	n.	结构；基础设施
oversee	[ˌəuvəˈsiː]	vt.	监督，监视
deplete	[diˈpliːt]	vt.	耗尽，使枯竭
crisis	[ˈkraisis]	n.	危机
specialized	[ˈspeʃəlaizd]	a.	专门的；专用的；专科的
discipline	[ˈdisiplin]	n.	学科；教学科目
draft	[drɑːft]	vt.	草拟，起草（文件）
facility	[fəˈsiliti]	n.	设备，装备，工具
roadway	[ˈrəudwei]	n.	车行道，道路
terrain	[təˈrein]	n.	地形；地貌；地势；地带
landscape	[ˈlændskeip]	n.	风景，景色
surveyor	[səˈveiə]	n.	测量员
specification	[ˌspesifiˈkeiʃən]	n.	规格；规格说明；具体说明；详述
urban	[ˈəːbən]	a.	城市的
administrator	[ədˈministreitə]	n.	管理人；行政人员
code	[kəud]	n.	法律，规章，章程
zoning	[ˈzəuniŋ]	n.	分区；分区制
regulation	[ˌregjuˈleiʃən]	n.	规章，规则；管理，控制，调节
consensus	[kənˈsensəs]	n.	（意见等）一致，一致同意
collaboration	[kəˌlæbəˈreiʃən]	n.	合作，协作

Civil Engineers Unit 1

facet ['fæsit]	n.		（问题等的）一个方面；（多面体的）面
single ['siŋgl]	a.		单一的；单个的
affect [ə'fekt]	vt.		影响
entire [in'taiə]	a.		全部的；整个的；完全的
immense [i'mens]	a.		巨大的；广大的
budget ['bʌdʒit]	n.		预算
criminal negligence			过失犯罪
at fault			有责任；有错
be up to			由某人决定；是某人的责任
wear and tear			损坏，损耗，用坏
run over			超过

Notes

1. Get your bearings on what it takes to become a successful civil engineer.

   搞清楚作为一个成功的土木工程师所要具备的素质。

   get one's bearings：确定自己的位置

2. We are able to take these expectations for granted thanks to the careful planning of a civil engineer.

   因为土木工程师的精心设计，人们才能够想当然地认为这些期望都会实现。

   take sth. for granted：认为某事属实。

   e. g. I take it for granted you have read this book. 我认为你一定读过这本书。

3. They figure out how the infrastructures we use, and the structures we build can be designed to function effectively.

   他们会搞清楚人们使用的基础设施以及所建的建筑物是如何有效地发挥作用。

   figure out：理解，弄明白。

   e. g. Have you figured out what's wrong with your car? 你找出你汽车的毛病了吗？

4. Structural engineering focuses on how structures such as buildings, tunnels, and bridges can be designed to support themselves, and to withstand wear and tear.

结构工程主要集中于如楼房、隧道、桥梁等结构如何设计，以支撑自身并经受损耗。

focus on：集中于某事物。

e. g. I'm so tired I can't focus(on anything)today. 今天我太累了，精神集中不起来。

5. It is up to you as a civil engineer to make sure that everyone else involved in a project's completion is not wasting his or her efforts on faulty design.

作为一个土木工程师，你有责任保证每一个涉及工程竣工的人员都没有在错误的设计上浪费时间。

be up to sb：是某人的责任或义务

e. g. It's up to us to help those in need. 我们有责任帮助那些有困难的人。

Exercises

Ⅰ. Answer the following questions according to the text.

1. What qualities do you need in order to become a successful civil engineer?
2. What are civil engineers supposed to do?
3. In addition to new projects, what are civil engineers hired to do? Why are they hired to do all these jobs?
4. Why job opportunities in civil engineering are plentiful even during the times of economic crisis?
5. How many major civil engineering disciplines are there? What are they?
6. If you are a construction engineer, what will your duties be?
7. What are you required to do as a civil engineer in any discipline?
8. Being a civil engineer means an immense amount of pressure on your success. Can you give any examples to explain?

Ⅱ. Translate the following terms into Chinese.

1. structural engineering
2. construction engineering
3. project site
4. employment contract
5. water resources engineering
6. environmental engineering
7. sanitary engineering
8. pollution control
9. waste management

10. public health

11. transportation engineering

12. geotechnical engineering

参考译文

土木工程师

职业指南

搞清楚作为一个成功的土木工程师所要具备的素质。

为了项目设计而进行的技术计算所必需的数学技能（30%）。

涉及工程建设的不同因素及其相互影响的相关知识（25%）。

向与项目相关的不同人员清楚地表达自己的想法或设计理念的交流能力（25%）。

在对最后期限有严格要求的工作领域有应付压力的能力，在压力和长期多任务的情况下解决问题的能力（20%）。

目标：土木工程师

人们对现代生活有着很多的期望。人们期望乘地铁到达目的地，期望下雨天道路不要雨水泛滥，期望在自己驾车通过的时候桥梁不要坍塌。因为土木工程师（如图1.1所示）的精心设计，人们才能够想当然地认为这些期望都会实现。

总之，土木工程师能让事情顺利实现。他们会搞清楚人们使用的基础设施以及所建的建筑物是如何有效地发挥作用。他们利用科学知识和数学原理，以及他们对于经济和环境因素的理解，来规划和监督一个工程的设计和施工。通常，土木工程师们会受雇于会对很多人产生影响的大型工程中。

图1.1　土木工程师的目标规划

除了设计新的项目，土木工程师们也受雇去帮助更新现有的工程。随着世界人口的增长，人们赖以生存的很多系统——例如供水、废物处理和交通网络——必须得以调整。全世界越来越多的人口就意味着更大的污染，更少的供人们使用的自然资源。土木工程师的任务就是要指出作为一种文明，人们如何发挥作用并发展而不会耗尽地球的资源，这就是为什么在这个领域的工作机遇很多，即便是在经济危机时期。事实上，土木工程领域的就业率预计会在下一个10年中增长18%。

虽然某些工程师(通常指"工地"工程师)在一个专门领域监督各个方面的工作，但主要的土木工程学科有6个。结构工程主要集中于如楼房、隧道、桥梁等结构如何设计，以支撑自身并经受损耗。施工工程主要是监督工程施工的各个方面：职责从施工工地的规划到供给的估算，还有起草雇佣合同。水资源工程主要集中在自然水资源的管理与收集方法上。环境工程(以前称作"卫生工程")主要集中在污染控制、废物处理、再循环系统，以及因此类设备的不足引起的潜在的公共健康问题。交通工程主要集中在计划、建设以及维护交通基础设施，如公路、铁路系统、机场、港口以及地铁系统。岩土工程主要集中在岩石、土壤、地形和其他地质构成对基础设施的影响。

学科不同，土木工程师的职责也有所不同。如果你是岩土或环境工程师，很多工作将在户外进行，和测量员一起研究工地的地形或土壤。如果你是结构工程师，你可能既在户外消除施工难题，又在室内写规划细则和合同书。对于市区项目，你的部分职责或许会包括与市区行政人员会面，和他们讨论某些诸如排水法规、分区法规、污染防治法以及社区协商结果等的问题。

不论在哪一个学科，作为一名土木工程师，都必须既要有实践性又要有创造性，都必须具备提供新的设计方案的科学与数学原则的实用性知识，还必须具有良好的交流能力，因为很多大型项目的建设要靠很多不同的人的合作。为了确保一项设计规划的各个方面能够协同合作，你还必须善于处理细节，能遵守最后期限，以及应付多重任务。

不像建筑师，他们通常设计的是影响部分人的单个建筑，而土木工程师设计的是会影响整个城市的基础设施。监督这样的大型项目会给工程师施加巨大的压力以便成功。如果项目失败，你会被追究责任，在最糟糕的情况下你会被以过失犯罪起诉。如果项目超过了预算或进度表，或者设计需要重新考虑，那么你必须要花额外的时间来解决这些问题。作为一个土木工程师，你有责任保证每一个涉及工程竣工的人员都没有在错误的设计上浪费时间。土木工程意味着要负很多的责任，你必须对自己的能力有十分的自信，而且要不知疲倦地投入工作中。土木工程师平均一周要工作标准的40个小时。然而，他们的工作日程又受到施工进度的影响而发生改变。

Reading Material: Make the Most of Your Journey

Winston Churchill once said, "We shape our buildings, thereafter they shape us." Since the human race began, this has been true. As time passes, we make our systems and products more advanced, thus advancing ourselves as a civilization. Those who work in engineering, mechanics, or architecture have some of the most important and exciting jobs because their work is at the forefront of this advancement. These forward-thinking professions are concerned with creating ways for our rapidly growing population to progress while continuing to live and thrive our planet.

While attention to detail is important in these careers, attention to the big picture is also important. To find success, you must be able to think a lot—not just about how your work will affect those around you now, but how it will affect the future of the human race as a whole. Employers, clients, and other professionals will be excited to work with you if you can tell that you are genuinely interested in making a better place, and that you are able to think on a large enough scale to do so.

If you want to pursue a career in engineering, mechanics, or architecture, you have to love the work, and also be patient on your path to job success. As famed architect Frank Lloyd Wright once said about his chosen field, "I know the price of success, dedication, hard work, and an unremitting devotion to the things you want to see happen." Just because you have a knack for gardening does not mean you will necessarily become a successful landscape architect overnight; if drawing maps is a hobby of yours. It does not mean you possess all the necessary skills to work as a professional cartographer just yet. In order to work in many of these job fields, you must be licensed, and you must sometimes obtain educational degrees before even applying to take the licensure exams. Just think about it the next time you are driving over the Golden Gate Bridge:

Aren't you glad the structural engineers involved in its design were required by law to know exactly what they were doing? Dedication and extreme enjoyment of the work at hand will help see you through these at times tedious requirements. If you are incredibly passionate about design, then taking some design classes to become legitimately qualified will be enjoyable learning experiences as opposed to mundane stepping-stones to be fulfilled in your career pursuit.

If you love what you do, you will also be able to find enjoyment even in the most stressful parts of your job. Financial motivation alone will not sustain you through long hours and difficult projects. Your paycheck will be steady for the most part, and you may even advance to a high-paying job, but you should not pursue a career in engineering, mechanics, or architecture only because you are aiming to get rich. Professionals who find success in engineering, mechanics, or architecture are people whose priorities lie more in environmental issues and human interests than in financial gain and material wealth.

New Words and Expressions

thereafter [ðɛərˈɑːftə]	ad.	之后，以后
mechanics [miˈkæniks]	n.	力学；机械学
thrive [θraiv]	vi.	茁壮成长；蓬勃发展；繁荣
pursue [pəˈsjuː]	vt.	追寻；追求；从事；进行
famed [feimd]	a.	著名的
dedication [dediˈkeiʃən]	n.	忠诚；奉献
unremitting [ˌʌnriˈmitiŋ]	a.	不放松的；不停止的；不间断的；坚持的
knack [næk]	n.	技巧；诀窍
overnight [ˌəuvəˈnait]	ad.	突然；很快
cartographer [kɑːˈtɔgrəfə]	n.	制图员
tedious [ˈtiːdiəs]	a.	令人厌倦的；烦人的
passionate [ˈpæʃənit]	a.	充满激情的；热切的，强烈的
legitimate [liˈdʒitimət]	a.	法定的；合法的；正当的；合理的
mundane [mʌnˈdein]	a.	平凡的；平淡的
motivation [ˌməutəˈveiʃən]	n.	动机；目的

motivation	[ˌməutə'veiʃən]	n.	动机；目的
sustain	[sə'stein]	vt.	保持；供养，维持；支持；经受
paycheck	['peitʃek]	n.	薪水支票，工资
priority	[prai'ɔriti]	n.	重点；优先考虑的事
landscape architect			园林技师
stepping-stone	['stepiŋˌstəun]	n.	踏脚石；方法，手段

Unit 2

Building Engineering

Text: Construction Engineering

Construction engineering concerns the planning and management of the construction of structures such as highways, bridges, airports, railroads, buildings, dams, and reservoirs (Fig. 2.1). Construction of such projects requires knowledge of engineering and management prin-

Fig. 2.1 Construction Projects

ciples and business procedures, economics and human behavior. Construction engineers engage in the design of temporary structures, quality assurance and quality control, building and site layout surveys, on site material testing, concrete mix design, cost estimating, planning and scheduling, safety engineering, materials procurement, and cost engineering and budgeting.

Construction engineering is differentiated from construction management from the standpoint of the level of mathematics, science and engineering used to analyze problems and design a construction process.

Work activities

Construction engineers have a wide range of responsibilities. Typically entry level construction engineers analyze reports and estimate project costs both in the office and in the field (Fig. 2.2). Other tasks may include analyzing maps, drawings, blueprints, aerial photography and other topographical information. Construction engineers also have to use computer software to design hydraulic systems and structures while following construction codes. Keeping a workplace safe is key to having a successful construction company. It is the construction engineer's job to make sure that everything is conducted correctly. In addition to safety, the construction engineer has to make sure that the site stays clean and sanitary. They have to make sure that there are no impediments in the way of the structure's planned location and must move any that exist. Finally, more seasoned construction engineers will assume the role of project management on a construction site and are involved heavily with the construction schedule and document control as well as budget and cost control. Their role on site is to provide construction information, including repairs, requests for information, change orders and payment applications to the managers and/or the owner's representatives.

Fig. 2.2 Construction Engineers

Skills

Construction engineers should have strong understanding for math and science, but many other skills are required, including critical thinking, listening, learning, problem solving, monitoring and decision making. Construction engineers have to be able to think about all aspects of a problem and listen to other's ideas so that they can learn everything about a project before it begins. During project construction they must solve the problems that they encounter using math and science. Construction Engineers must maintain project control of labor and equipment for safety, to ensure the project is on schedule and monitor quality control. When a problem occurs, it is the construction engineer who will create and enact a solution.

Abilities

Construction engineers need different abilities to do their job. They must have the ability to reason, convey instructions to others, comprehend multi-variables, anticipate problems, comprehend verbal, written and graphic instructions, organize data sets, speak clearly, visualize in 4D time-space and understand Virtual Design and Construction methods.

Educational Requirements

A typical construction engineering curriculum is a mixture of engineering mechanics, engineering design, construction management and general science and mathematics. This usually leads to a Bachelor of Science degree. The B. S. degree along with some construction experience is sufficient for most entry level construction engineering jobs. Graduate school may be an option for those who want to go further in depth of the construction and engineering subjects taught at the undergraduate level. In most cases, construction engineering graduates look to either civil engineering, engineering management, or business administration as a possible graduate degree. For authority to approve any final designs of public projects(and most any project), a construction engineer must have a professional engineers(P. E.)license. To obtain a P. E. license, the Fundamentals of Engineering exam and Principles and Practice in Engineering Exam must be passed, and education and experience requirements met.

New Words and Expressions

engineering [ˌendʒɪˈnɪərɪŋ]	n.	工程(学)，工程师行业
principle [ˈprɪnsəpl]	n.	原则，原理；准则，规范
reservoir [ˈrezəvwaː]	n.	水库；储藏；汇集
temporary [ˈtempərəri]	a.	临时的，暂时的，短时间的
assurance [əˈʃuərəns]	n.	保证，担保；确信；把握，信心
scheduling [ˈskedʒuːlɪŋ]	n.	时序安排；行程安排

procurement	[prə'kjuəmənt]	n.	获得；采购
budgeting	['bʌdʒitiŋ]	n.	预定；预算
differentiate	[,difə'renʃieit]	vt. & vi.	区分，区别，辨别
analyze	['ænəlaiz]	vt.	分析，分解，解释
standpoint	['stændpɔint]	n.	立场；观点
blueprint	['bluː'print]	n.	蓝图，设计图
aerial	['ɛəriəl]	a.	空气的，空中的
topographical	[,tɔpə'græfikəl]	n.	地志的；地形学的
hydraulic	[hai'drɔːlik]	a.	液力的，液压的
sanitary	['sænitəri]	a.	清洁的，卫生的，保健的
impediment	[im'pedimənt]	n.	妨碍、阻碍某事物进展或活动的人或物；身体上的某类残疾，缺陷
seasoned	['siːzənd]	a.	成熟的；老练的
encounter	[in'kauntə]	vt.	遇到，遭遇；偶然碰到，邂逅
monitor	['mɔnitə]	vt.	监测，检测；监听，监视
convey	[kən'vei]	vt.	表达，转达；运输；运送
variable	['vɛəriəbl]	n. a.	可变因素；变数 变化的，可变的，易变的
anticipate	[æn'tisipeit]	vt.	预期，期望，预料，预先考虑到
verbal	['vəːbəl]	a.	口头的，词语的，言语的，字句的
virtual	['vəːtjuəl]	a.	实质上的，事实上的，实际上的
curriculum	[kə'rikjuləm]	n.	课程
administration	[əd,minis'treiʃən]	n.	管理，经营，支配；实行，执行
professional	[prə'feʃənəl]	a.	职业的，专业的；内行的，有经验的

license ['laisəns]	n.	许可证，执照，牌照
construction engineering		建筑工程
engage in		参加，从事，忙于
differentiate from		指出…与…有区别
aerial photography		空中摄影，空中照相术
on schedule		按照预定时间，按时间表，准时
bachelor of science		理学学士
in depth		深入地，全面地
civil engineering		土木工程

Notes

1. Construction engineers engage in the design of temporary structures, quality assurance and quality control, building and site layout surveys, on site material testing, concrete mix design, cost estimating, planning and scheduling, safety engineering, materials procurement, cost engineering and budgeting.

   建筑工程师参与临时建筑物的设计、质量保证和控制、建筑和工地布局测量、现场材料检验、混凝土配合比设计、成本估算、计划与进度安排、安全工程、材料采购、成本管理和预算。

   engage in sth.：参加或从事某事。

   e. g. I have no time to engage in gossip. 我无暇闲聊。

2. Finally, more seasoned construction engineers will assume the role of project management on a construction site...

   最后，经验丰富的建筑工程师要在建筑工地承担起项目管理的角色……

   本句中的 seasoned 指有丰富经验的。

3. The B. S. degree along with some construction experience is sufficient for most entry level construction engineering jobs.

   对于大多数基础水平的建筑工程工作而言，理学学士学位再加上一定的施工经验就足够了。

Exercises

I. Answer the following questions according to the text.

1. What is construction engineering about?
2. What do construction engineers engage in?
3. What are tasks of an entry level engineer?
4. What is key to running a successful construction company?
5. What role are more seasoned construction engineers supposed to assume? What tasks are they involved with?
6. What kind of skills are construction engineers required to have?
7. What abilities are construction engineers required to have?
8. If a construction engineer wants to have a Bachelor of Science degree, what subject is he/she supposed to learn?
9. If a construction engineer wants to go further in depth of the construction and engineering subjects taught at a undergraduate level, what is his/her option?
10. If the final design of a project is to be approved by authority, what qualification is a construction engineer required to have?

II. Translate the following terms into Chinese.

1. construction engineering
2. quality assurance and quality control
3. construction management
4. construction codes
5. construction schedule and document control
6. project construction
7. verbal, written and graphic instructions
8. civil engineering

参考译文

建筑工程

建筑工程关乎高速公路、桥梁、机场、铁路、楼房、大坝和水库等建筑物施工的计划和管理(图2.1)。这些项目的施工需要工程学、管理原则、商业程序、经济学和人类行为的知识。建筑工程师参与临时建筑物的设计、质量保证和控制、建筑和工地布局测量、现场材料检验、混凝土配合比设计、成本估算、计划与进度安排、安全工程、材料采购、成本管理和预算。

图2.1 建筑项目

从用来分析问题和设计施工过程中使用的数学、科学和工程学的情况的角度来看,建筑工程与建筑施工管理是有区别的。

工作活动

图2.2 建筑工程师

建筑工程师肩负着一系列的责任。通常基础水平的建筑工程师要在办公室和工地分析各种报告以及估算项目成本(图2.2)。其他的任务还包括分析地图、施工图、工程蓝图、航空摄影测量以及其他地形信息。在遵循建筑法规的同时,建筑工程师还要用电子计算机软件设计液压系统和建筑物。保持工作场所的安全是一个成功的建筑公司运营的关键。建筑工程师的工作就是要确保每一项操作都要正确。除了安全,建筑工程师还要确保工地的整洁与卫生。他们必须要保证在建筑物计划位置没有任何障碍物,如果有的话必须要移走。最后，经验丰富的建筑工程师要在建筑工地承担起项目管理的角色，并大规模参与施工进度、施工文件管理以及预算与成本控制。他们在工地上的角色是提供施工资料，包括修葺、资料请求、变更单、向经理和业主代表或向业主代表提出的支付申请。

技能

建筑工程师应该对数学和科学有很强的理解力，但是也要求他们掌握其他的技能，包括批判性思考的能力、听的能力、学习能力、解决问题的能力、监督以及作出决定的能力。建筑工程师必须能够考虑到问题的各个方面并且听取别人意见，以便在项目开始之前就能对它了如指掌。在项目施工期间，他们必须用数学和科学知识解决遇到的问题。建筑工程师为了安全起见必须坚持对劳力和设备的项目控制，确保工程按计划进行并监督质量管理。当有问题出现时，建筑工程师就应该找到并实施解决方案。

能力

建筑工程师要做好他们的工作需要不同的能力。他们必须具有思考能力，向别人传达指令的能力，理解多种可变因素的能力，预见问题的能力，理解口头、书面和图表指令的能力，编组数据集的能力，清楚表达的能力，四维时间和空间想象的能力，以及理解虚拟设计和施工方法的能力。

学历要求

典型的建筑工程课程包含了工程力学、工程设计、施工管理，以及基础科学和数学。学完这些课程就能拿到理学学士学位。对于大多数基础水平的建筑工程工作而言，理学学士学位再加上一定的施工经验就足够了。如果想对本科阶段学过的建筑和工程学科进行更进一步的、深入的学习，研究生院也许是不错的选择。在大多数情况下，建筑工程专业的研究生都希望以土木工程、工程管理或商业管理作为他们可能取得的研究生学位。建筑工程师必须具有职业工程师许可证，以便管理机构批准任何公共项目（几乎是所有项目）的最终设计。要想获得职业工程师许可证，就必须通过工程基础考试和工程原理与实践考试，并达到学历和工作经验的要求。

Reading Material: Different Types of Buildings

Man requires different types of buildings for his activities: houses, bungalows and flats for his living; hospitals and health centers for his health; schools, colleges and universities for his education; banks, shops, offices, buildings and factories for work; railway buildings, bus stations and air terminals for transportation; clubs, theatres and cinema houses for recreation, and temples, mosques, churches, dharmsala etc. for worship. Each type of the above buildings has its own requirements. The above building activities are an important indicator of the country's social progress.

Houses, bungalows, flats, huts etc. provide shelter for man. The first hut with bamboos and leaves can be taken as the first civil engineering construction carried out to satisfy the needs for a shelter. Before that, caves were his early abode. The history of development of housing facilities reveals that man has been molding his environment throughout the ages, for more comfortable living. India still has many old cave temples with halls and rooms having beautiful carvings. Egyptians constructed Great Pyramids. The Greeks developed a style of proportions of building elements; these proportions are known as the Orders of Architecture. Romans developed arches for vaults and domes. They used pozzolana sand, mortar, plaster and concrete. During the Gothic period of architecture (1100—1500 A. D.) churches with pointed arches and the ribs supporting masonry vaults were constructed. The arched ribs were supported by stone pillars strengthened by buttresses. These structures led to the idea of framed structures.

The period from 1750 A. D. onwards is known as the period of Modern Architecture. Due to economic pressure after the war, and due to industrial development, many new methods and materials of construction were developed. The use of reinforced concrete construction triggered the rapid development of modern architecture. Functional structural components such as columns, chajjas, canopies, R. C. C. slabs became increasingly popular because of the increased speed in construction. Use of plywood, glass, decorative etc. helped the designers to make the new structures look more elegant.

The building design has traditionally been the responsibility of the architect, though the building construction has been the responsibility of the civil engineer. Also, the structural designs of the building are the responsibility of the civil engineer. On small projects, a civil engineer may sometimes be entrusted with the architectural design work, along with structural designs. The main considerations in architectural design of buildings for all purposes are as follows:

(1) Climate and its effect.

(2) People and their requirements.

(3) Materials for construction and method of construction.

(4) Regulations and bye-laws of sanctioning authority.

Types of Buildings

National Building Code of India (SP: 7 – 1970) defines the buildings, "any structure for whatsoever purpose and of whatsoever materials constructed and every part thereof whether used as human habitation or not and includes foundations, plinth, walls, floors, roofs, chimneys, plumbing and building services, fixed platforms, verandah, balcony cornice or projection, part of a building or any thing affixed thereto or any wall enclosing or intended to enclose any land or space and signs and outdoor display structures". Tents, shamianas and tarpaulin shelters are not considered as building.

According to the National Building Code of India (1970), buildings are classified, based on occupancy, as follows:

(1) Residential buildings.
(2) Educational buildings.
(3) Institutional buildings.
(4) Assembly buildings.
(5) Business buildings.
(6) Mercantile buildings.
(7) Industrial buildings.
(8) Storage buildings.
(9) Hazardous buildings.

New Words and Expressions

mosque ['mɔsk]	n.	清真寺，伊斯兰教寺院
worship ['wəːʃip]	vi.	做礼拜
	vt.	崇拜
bungalow ['bʌŋgləu]	n.	平房；单层小屋
abode [ə'bəud]	n.	住所，公寓
proportion [prə'pɔːʃən]	n.	均衡，协调；比例
vault [vɔːlt]	n.	柱，圆柱

dome [dəum]	n.	拱顶
pozzolana [ˌpɔtsəˈlɑːnə]	n.	火山灰（可用作水泥原料）
mortar [ˈmɔːtə]	n.	砂浆，灰浆；房产
Gothic [ˈgɔθik]	a. n.	哥特式的 哥特式
buttress [ˈbʌtris]	n.	扶壁，扶垛
trigger [ˈtrigə]	vt.	引发，引起
canopy [ˈkænəpiː]	n.	华盖，罩篷
plywood [ˈplaiˌwud]	n.	胶合板，合板，夹板
verandah [vəˈrændə]	n.	阳台
cornice [ˈkɔːnis]	n.	檐口
tarpaulin [tɑːˈpɔːlin]	n.	防水帆布，防水帆布罩
occupancy [ˈɔkjupənsi]	n.	占有，使用
hazardous [ˈhæzədəs]	a.	冒险的，有危险的
lead to		导致，引起
due to		因……而产生，（作为结果）发生
be entrusted with		受委托做某事

Unit 3

Building Components

Text: Components of a Building

All buildings have the same components such as foundation, walls, floors and roof. In addition, we have to decorate them with plaster, paint, etc, to make them aesthetically beautiful. These items of building works are called civil works. Water and electricity have also to be supplied to the buildings to make them habitable. These items are called building services. In this article, we will briefly examine the various components of civil works.

Components of a Building: Civil Works

The important parts of an ordinary are shown in Figures 3.1 and 3.2. They are as follows:
(1) Foundation.
(2) Plinth.
(3) Walls and columns.
(4) Floors.
(5) Lintels and *chajjas*.
(6) Roof.

(7) Doors and windows.

(8) Stairs and lifts.

(9) Finishing work(plastering and painting).

(10) Building services.

(11) Fencing and external works.

A building can be divided into substructure(foundation) and superstructure, the plinth being the dividing line between them. In building construction, we study how the civil works are carried out in the field after they have been planned by an architect and structurally designed by an engineer.

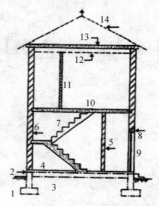

1 – Foundation, 2 – Plinth, 3 – Basement filling, 4 – Ground floor, 5 – Internal wall, 6 – Extenal wall, 7 – Staircase, 8 – Lintel, 9 – Door, 10 – Upper floor, 11 – Partition wall, 12 – Ceiling, 13 – Flat roof, 14 – Sloping roof

Fig. 3.1 Parts of a Building

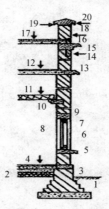

1 – Foundation, 2 – Hard core(Basement filling), 3 – Plinth, 4 – Ground floor, 5 – Still, 6 – Window, 7 – Reveal(revealed vertical wall on the sides of door or window frame as inner reveal and outer reveal), 8 – Jamb(vertical wall on both sides of doorway or window opening), 9 – Lintel, 10 – Corbel, 11 – Ceiling, 12 – Upper floor, 13 – String course with throating, 14 – Frieze(stone course below cornice), 15 – Cornice, 16 – Blocking course, 17 – Terracing, 18 – Parapet, 19 – DPC under coping, 20 – Coping

Fig. 3.2 Section Through a Wall

We should be aware that there are many aspects that are involved in the preliminary planning and design of the building. For example, an architect specializes in the following work:

(1) Planning the orientation, layout and dimension of the rooms of the building.

(2) The preparation of the features to make the building attractive.

Work of this nature for small buildings may be taken by non-architects also. However, the construction of a building should always be carried out under the supervision of a qualified person. We will now briefly examine the construction of the different components of buildings.

Construction of Foundation

Foundation is a very important part of a building. Foundation engineering is a special subject. A foundation engineer should know how to examine the soil profile and arrive at a suitable foundation. The following are some of the different types of foundation generally used:

(1) Strip foundation (shallow foundations).

(2) Footing foundation (shallow foundations).

(3) Raft foundation (shallow foundation).

(4) Pile foundation (deep foundation).

(5) Pier foundation (deep foundation).

In framed construction, we use footings as the foundation for the column and the brickwork for walls starts from grade beams connecting columns. (Grade beams on underreamed piles are also called capping beams.)

Construction of Plinth

Plinth is the dividing line between the substructure and superstructure. Thus, the projecting part of the wall above the ground level to a floor level is the plinth. It is capped by a beam called plinth beam. The provision of a plinth beam and damp-proof course at plinth level are very important in building construction. The plinth is usually kept at least 45cm (1.5ft) above the general ground level of the building.

Construction of Walls and Columns

Walls are mostly made of masonry. It may be of brick, blockwork, stonework and so on. Hence, a study of these different types of masonry is made under this head. Construction of different types of walls such as load bearing walls, partition walls, etc. is also to be studied under this head. Buildings may also be constructed as a framed structure with columns and footings and then infilled. Most of the flats and high-rise buildings are built this way. In many places in the masonry, we use arches and lintels. Their study also forms part of masonry construction.

Construction of Floors

We have to study the details of the construction of the ground floors constructed on the ground as well as the top floors. Nowadays these top floors are usually made of reinforced concrete. A detailed study of concrete work, formwork and placing of steel reinforcement comes under this head. Different types of floor finishes for these floors are also to be studied.

Construction of Roof

Roof is an important part of all buildings. The most important item in housing is to have a "roof over one's head". Depending on the finances available and also the climatic conditions, we can have different kinds of roofs. Roofs can be sloped or flat. Many types of roofs and roofing materials are available nowadays. A study of these is absolutely essential for a building engineer. Another important study is how to make the roofs waterproof, heatproof or weatherproof.

Fabrication of Doors and Windows

Openings are necessary in buildings for passages inside and outside the buildings. We also need the windows for lighting and ventilation. A detailed study of doors and windows is an important part of building construction as the expenditure on this item alone can go up to 15 to 20 percent of the total cost of the civil works. Traditionally doors and windows were made of woods and hence this work is sometimes referred to woodwork in buildings. Other woodwork like provision of cupboards is also important but it comes under the subject of interior decoration.

Stairs and Lifts

Nowadays most buildings are made more than one storey high. A knowledge of various elements of the staircase and the construction of simple staircase is essential to all those involved in building construction. Study of the layout and design of ornamental staircases is a special subject. Usually vertical transportation devices like electric lifts are to be provided in buildings having more than four floors including the ground floor. We must also be familiar with these devices.

Building Finishes

The final appearance of the building depends very much on its finishing. We have to deal with the following:

(1) Plastering and pointing.

(2) Painting of walls, woodwork, grillwork and so on.

It is essential that we have a knowledge of the finishing to be used on the various materials of construction such as plaster, wood, metals and so on.

New Words and Expressions

foundation [faunˈdeiʃən]	n.		地基,房基
plaster [ˈplɑːstə]	n.		灰泥,石膏
aesthetically [iːsˈθetikəli]	ad.		审美地,美学观点上地
habitable [ˈhæbitəbəl]	a.		适于居住的
lintel [ˈlintl]	n.		楣,过梁
column [ˈkɔləm]	n.		柱,圆柱
plinth [plinθ]	n.		底座,基座
preliminary [priˈliminəri]	a.		初步的,预备的,开端的
orientation [ˌɔːrienˈteiʃn]	n.		方向,目标
profile [ˈprəufail]	n.		纵断面,纵剖面图
pile [pail]	n.		桩,堆
pier [piə]	n.		柱子,桥墩,墙墩
geotechnical [ˌdʒiəuˈteknikəl]	a.		土工的
curriculum [kəˈrikjuləm]	n.		课程
anti-termite [ˌæntiˈtəːmait]	n.		防白蚁

partition [pɑː'tiʃən]	n.	分隔物，隔墙
ventilation [venti'leiʃən]	n.	空气流通，通风设备；通风方法
grillwork ['grilwəːk]	n.	格型图案
in addition		另外，此外
be aware		意识到，注意
carry out		实行，执行；完成，实现
deal with		论述，涉及
reinforced concrete		钢筋混凝土
be familiar with		对……熟悉

Notes

1. A building can be divided into substructure (foundation) and superstructure, the plinth being the dividing line between them.
   一座建筑物可以分为下部结构(地基)和上部结构，以柱基作为分界线。

2. Thus, the projecting part of the wall above the ground level to a floor level is the plinth.
   因此，地面以上至楼面的突出部分便是柱基。
   projecting 表示突出的。

3. Hence, a study of these different types of masonry is made under this head.
   因此，此处对不同类型的石砌工程予以研究。
   under this head 指在此标题下。

4. Depending on the finances available and also the climatic conditions, we can have different kinds of roofs. 鉴于建设资金以及气候条件等因素，会有不同类型的屋顶。

5. A detailed study of doors and windows is an important part of building construction as the expenditure on this item alone can go up to 15 to 20 percent of the total cost of the civil works.
   民用建筑中，只是门窗的建造费用就可达到建筑总费用的15%～20%，因此对门窗的建造进行详细研究是非常重要的。
   as 表示原因，the expenditure on this item alone 只是在这方面的花费。

Exercises

Ⅰ. Answer the following questions according to the text.

1. Why do people decorate their buildings with plaster, paint etc.?
2. What is the difference between civil works and building services?
3. What is the dividing line between substructure(foundation) and superstructure?
4. According to the article, what kind of work can be taken by non-architects?
5. Can you name some of the different types of foundation generally used?
6. What is another name of grade beams on underream piles?
7. In what way are most of the flats and high-rise buildings built?
8. What are top floors nowadays usually made of?
9. In housing, what is the most important item?
10. Are vertical transportation devices like electric lifts are to be provided in buildings having more than six floors including the ground floor?

Ⅱ. Translate the following terms into Chinese.

1. civil work
2. walls and columns
3. soil profile
4. hard core
5. damp-proof course
6. blocking course
7. grade beam
8. interior decoration
9. load bearing wall
10. concrete work

参考译文

建筑物的构造

所有建筑物都有诸如地基、墙体、地板和屋顶这些相同构造。此外，人们还须使用石膏、油漆等材料对房屋进行装修，使其美观，这些建筑工程项目就叫土建工程。建筑物还须配备水电以适于居住，此类项目称为屋宇设备。本文将简要考察土建工程的各个构造。

建筑物的构造：土建工程

图3.1和图3.2所示的是一般建筑物的重要构造，分别如下。

（1）地基。

（2）柱基。

（3）墙体和柱体。

（4）地板。

（5）门楣和挑檐。

（6）屋顶。

（7）门和窗。

（8）楼梯和电梯。

（9）精整工程（抹石膏和喷漆）。

（10）屋宇设备。

（11）围栏和外部工程。

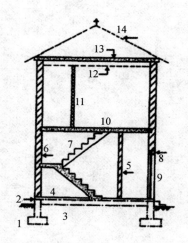

1—地基，2—柱基，3—地下室填充物，4—基层，5—内墙，6—外墙，7—楼梯，8—门楣，9—门，10—上层楼面，11—隔间墙，12—顶棚，13—平顶，14—斜面屋顶

图3.1 建筑物构件

一座建筑物可以分为下部结构（地基）和上部结构，以柱基作为分界线。在房屋建筑中，人们要研究的是建筑工程在由建筑师完成平面设计并由工程师完成结构设计后如何在现场进行施工。

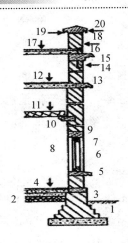

1—地基，2—碎石填层（地下室填充物），3—柱基，4—基层，5—蒸馏室，6—窗户，7—门窗框（门框或窗框两侧的垂直墙面，分内侧壁和外侧壁），8—门窗侧壁（门口和窗口两边的垂直墙体），9—门楣，10—枕梁，11—顶棚，12—上层楼面，13—滴水槽，14—雕带（飞檐下部的石制部分），15—飞檐，16—檐头墙，17—露台，18—护栏，19—防潮墙盖，20—顶盖

图 3.2 墙体切面

应当注意，在建筑物的最初规划和设计中会涉及许多方面的问题，例如，建筑师专门从事下列工作。

（1）规划建筑物房间的方位、布局和大小规格。

（2）创构凸显建筑物魅力的特征。

对一些小型建筑，此类性质的工作也可由非建筑师来完成。但是，建筑物的施工建造一定要在具有资质的人的监督下进行。人们将简要考查建筑物不同构件的建造。

地基的建造

地基是建筑物非常重要的一个部分。地基工程是一个特殊的工程项目。地基工程师应当知道如何检测土层剖切面并获得适当的地基。下列是几类常用的、不同类型的地基。

（1）条形地基（浅地基）。

（2）台阶式地基（浅地基）。

（3）板式地基（浅地基）。

（4）打桩地基（深地基）。

（5）墩式地基（深地基）。

在框架结构建筑中，用台阶式地基作为支柱的地基和砖砌结构的地基，墙体从连接支柱的地基梁开始建造。（**建在扩孔管道上的地基梁也叫柱顶梁**）。

柱基的建造

柱基是建筑物上下部结构的分界线。因此，地面以上至楼面的突出部分便是柱基。柱基被横梁封盖，这道横梁被称为基柱梁。在建筑物建造中，基柱梁的作用以及基柱的防水构件是非常重要的。基柱至少要高于建筑物总体地面标高45cm(1.5ft)。

墙体和柱子的建造

墙体大多数是石砌的，有可能是砖、预制砌块、石料等。因此，此处对不同类型的石砌工程予以研究，对像承重墙、间隔墙等不同类型的墙体的建造也予以研究。对建筑物也可先建成带有柱子和台阶式地基的框架结构，然后再进行内填性建造。大多数公寓楼和高层建筑一般是用这种方式建造的。在石砌工程中，许多地方使用圆拱和门楣。他们的研究也构成了石砌工程的一部分。

楼面地板的建造

对地面基层和顶层的建造细节，人们都要进行研究。当今建筑的顶楼通常用钢筋混凝土建造。该部分对混凝土工程、模板及加放强化钢条的详细情况进行研究，同时对不同楼层的地板装修也予以研究。

屋顶建造

屋顶对于所有建筑物来说都是很重要的一个部分。在住房中，最重要的一项内容便是"头上有个屋顶"。鉴于建设资金以及气候条件等因素，会有不同类型的屋顶。屋顶可以是平顶的，也可是斜顶的。当今的建筑物有着很多种类型的屋顶，也用到很多种材料。对于一名建筑工程师来说，这些方面的研究绝对是很重要的。另一项重要研究便是如何建造防水、防热和耐风雨的屋顶。

门窗的制作

用以建筑物内外通行开口的建造是不可或缺的。同时，还需要窗户以用来采光和通风。民用建筑中，只是门窗的建造费用就可达到建筑总费用的15%~20%，因此对门窗的建造进行详细研究是非常重要的。传统的门窗均为木制的，因此在建筑中，这项工作有时就是指木工活。其他像橱柜之类的木工活也很重要，但这些都属于室内装修的范畴。

楼梯和电梯

当今的大多数建筑物都是多层的。对楼梯的组成部分以及简捷楼梯的建造有一定的认识,对于涉足建筑工程的人们是很有必要的。装饰性楼梯的布局和设计是一个特别的问题。通常,在包括基层在内超过四层的建筑中,都会提供像电梯这类垂直运送装置。对这些装置,人们也应当通晓。

建筑物的精整

建筑物的最后外观很大程度上取决于精整装饰。一般需要处理下列事项。
(1) 灰涂和勾缝。
(2) 墙面上漆、木工、打格等。
了解建筑物精整中所使用的各种材料是很重要的,比如石膏、木料、金属等。

Reading Material: Beijing Siheyuan

The siheyuan (Fig. 3.3) is a historical type of residence that was commonly founded throughout China, most famously in Beijing. In English, siheyuan are sometimes referred to Chinese quadrangles. The name literally means a courtyard surrounded by four buildings. Throughout Chinese history, the siheyuan composition is the basic pattern used for residences, palaces, temples, monasteries, family, businesses and government offices. In ancient times, a spacious siheyuan would be occupied by a single, usually large and extended family, signifying wealth and prosperity.

The four buildings of a siheyuan are normally positioned along the north-south and east-west axes. The building positioned to the north and facing the south is considered as the main house. The buildings adjoining the main house and facing east and west are called side houses. The northern, eastern and western buildings are connected by beautifully decorated pathways. These passages serve as shelters from the sunshine during the day, and provide a cool place to appreciate the view of the courtyard at night. The building that faces north is known as the opposite house. Behind the northern building, there would often be a separate backside building, the only place where two-story buildings are allowed to be constructed for the traditional siheyuan.

Fig. 3.3 Beijing Siheyuan

The entrance gate (Fig. 3.4), usually painted vermilion and with copper door knockers on it, is usually at the southeastern corner. Normally, there is a screen wall inside the gate, for privacy; superstition holds that it also protects the house from evil spirits. A pair of stone lions are often placed outside the gate. Some large siheyuan compounds would have two or more layers of courtyards and even private gardens attached to them. Such is a sign of wealth and status in ancient times.

The courtyard dwellings are built according to the traditional concepts of the five elements that are believed to compose the universe, and the eight diagrams of divination. The gate is made at the southeast corner which is the "wind" corner, and the main house is built on the north side which is believed to belong to "water" —an element to prevent fire.

Fig. 3.4 The Entrance Gate of a Beijing Siheyuan

The layout of a simple courtyard represents traditional Chinese morality and Confucian ethics. In Beijing, four buildings in a single courtyard receive different amounts of sunlight. The northern main building receives the most, thus serves as the living room and bedroom of the owner or head of the family. The eastern and western side buildings receive less, and serve as the rooms for children or less important members of the family. The southern building receives the least sunlight, and usually functions as a reception room and the servants' dwelling, or where the family would gather to relax, eat or study. The backside building is for unmarried daughters and female servants: because unmarried girls are not allowed direct exposure to the public, they occupy the most secluded building in the siheyuan.

A more detailed and further stratified Confucian order was followed in ancient China. The main house in the north was assigned to the eldest member of the family, i. e. the head of the family, usually grandparents. If the main house had enough rooms, a central room would serve as a shrine for ancestral worship. When the head of the household had concubines, the wife would reside in the room to the eastern end of the main house, while the concubines would reside in the room to the western end of the main house. The eldest son of the family and his wife would reside in the western side house, while the younger son and his wife would reside in the eastern side house. If a grandson was fully grown, he would reside in the opposite house in the south. Unmarried daughters would always reside in the backside building behind the main house.

Though from antiquity, a siheyuan is a practically sound, engineered structure. Northwestern walls are usually higher than the other walls to protect the inside buildings from the harsh winds blowing across northern China in the winter. Eaves curve downward, so that rainwater will flow along the curve rather than drop straight down. The rooftop is ridged to provide shade in the summer while retain warmth in the winter.

A siheyuan offers space, comfort, quiet and privacy. Siheyuan walls provide security as well as protection against dust and storms. With plants, rocks, and flowers, the yard is also a garden, and acts like an open-air living room. The veranda divides the courtyard into several big and small spaces that are not very distant from each other. Family members talk with each other here, creating a cordial atmosphere.

Recently, a modern version of siheyuan has been developed as a villa product in large scale planned residential communities of China. These new siheyuan are located in the new housing development areas of Beijing.

New Words and Expressions

literally ['litərəli]	ad.	逐字地；照字面地
quadrangle ['kwɔdræŋgl]	n.	四边形，四方院子
composition [ˌkɔmpə'ziʃən]	n.	构图；构成，成分
monastery ['mɔnəstəri]	n.	修道院
axes ['æksiːz]	n.	轴
adjoin [ə'dʒɔin]	vt. & vi.	邻近，毗连
vermilion [və'miljən]	n.	朱红色；鲜红色
	a.	朱红色的；鲜红色的
knocker ['nɔkə]	n.	门环
superstition [ˌsjuːpə'stiʃən]	n.	迷信，迷信行为
divination [ˌdivi'neiʃən]	n.	预言
secluded [si'kluːdid]	a.	与世隔绝的，隐退的，隐居的
stratify ['strætifai]	vt.	（使）分层，成层
shrine [ʃrain]	n.	圣地，圣坛，神圣场所
ancestral [æn'sestrəl]	a.	祖先的，祖宗传下来的
concubine ['kɔŋkjubain]	n.	妾，妃子
antiquity [æn'tikwiti]	n.	古老，年代久远，古物，古代
eaves ['iːvz]	n.	屋檐
ridge [ridʒ]	vi.	成脊状
veranda [və'rændə]	n.	阳台；游廊；走廊
villa ['vilə]	n.	别墅，公馆
siheyuan		四合院
main house		正房

side houses	厢房
pathways	廊
opposite house	倒座房
backside building	后罩房
screen wall	影壁
copper door knockers	铜门环
the five elements	（金木水火土）五行
the eight diagrams of divination	八卦占卜

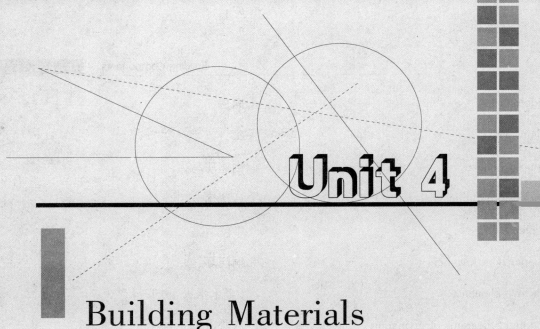

Unit 4

Building Materials

Text: Concrete as a Structural Material

Concrete is the most widely used construction material in the world, and its popularity can be attributed to two aspects. First, concrete is used for many different structures, such as dams, pavements, building frames, or bridges, much more than any other construction material. Second, the amount of concrete used is much more than any other material. Its worldwide production exceeds that of steel by a factor of 10 in tonnage and by more than a factor of 30 in volume.

In a concrete structure, there are two commonly used structural materials: concrete and steel. A structural material is a material that carries not only its self-weight, but also the load passing from other members.

Steel is manufactured under carefully controlled conditions, always in a highly sophisticated plant; the properties of every type of steel are determined in a laboratory and described in a manufacturer's certificate. Thus, the designer of a steel structure need only specify the steel complying with a relevant standard, and the constructor needs only to ensure that the correct steel is used and that connections between the individual steel members are properly executed.

On the other hand, concrete is produced in a cruder way and its quality varies considerably. Even the quality of cement, the binder of concrete, is guaranteed by the manufacturer in a manner similar to that of steel; however, the quality of concrete is hardly guaranteed because of many other factors, such as aggregates, mixing procedures, and skills of the operators of concrete production, placement, and consolidation.

It is possible to obtain concrete of specified quality from a ready-mix supplier, but, even in this case, it is only the raw materials that are bought for a construction job. Transporting, placing, and above all, compacting greatly influence the quality of cast concrete structure. Moreover, unlike the case of steel, the choice of concrete mixes is virtually infinite and therefore the selection has to be made with a sound knowledge of the properties and behavior of concrete. It is thus the competence of the designer and specifier that determines the potential qualities of concrete, and the competence of the supplier and the contractor that controls the actual quality of concrete in the finished structure. It follows that they must be thoroughly conversant with the properties of concrete and with concrete making and placing.

In a concrete structure, concretes mainly carry the compressive force and shear force, while the steel carries the tension force. Moreover, concrete usually provides stiffness for structures to keep them stable.

Concretes have been widely used to build various structures. High-strength concrete has been used in many tall building constructions. In Hong Kong, grade 80 concrete (80MPa) was utilized in the columns of the tallest building in the region. As shown in Figure 4.1, the 88-story International Finance Center was built in 2003 and stands 415m (1362ft) tall.

Fig. 4.1　International Finance Center, Hong Kong

Concrete has also been used in bridge construction. Figure 4.2 shows the recently built Sutong Bridge that spans the Yangtze River in China between Nantong and Changshu, a satellite city of Suzhou in Jiangsu province. It is a cable-stayed bridge with the longest main span, 1088 meters, in the world. Its two side spans are 300m(984ft) each, and there are also four small cable spans.

Fig. 4.2　The Sutong Bridge in Suzhou, Jiangsu

Dams are other popular application fields for concrete. The first major concrete dams, the Hoover Dam and the Grand Coulee Dam, were built in the 1930s and they are still standing. The largest dam ever built is the Three Gorges Dam in Hubei province, as shown in Figure 4.3. The total concrete used for the dam was over 22 million cubic meter.

Fig. 4.3　Three Gorges Dam, Hubei

Concrete has also been used to build high-speed railways. Shinkansen, the world's first contemporary high-volume(initially 12-car maximum), "high-speed rail", was built in Japan in 1964. In Europe, high-speed rail was introduced during the International Transport Fair in Munich in June 1965. Nowadays, high-speed rail construction is blooming in China. By the end of 2013, Chinese high-speed railway operating mileage of 11,000 kilometers, ranking first in the world, accounting for half of the world's total mileage. Figure 4.4 shows a high-speed rail system in China.

Fig. 4.4 High-speed Rail

In addition, concrete has been widely applied in the construction of airport runways, tunnels, highways, pipelines, and oil platforms. As of now, the annual world consumption of concrete has reached a value such that if concrete were edible, every person on earth would have 2000kg per year to "eat". You may wonder why concrete has become so popular.

New Words and Expressions

structural	[ˈstrʌktʃərəl]	a.	结构的，建筑的，构造的
pavement	[ˈpeivmənt]	n.	铺过的道路，人行道
tonnage	[ˈtʌnidʒ]	n.	吨位，总吨数，船舶吨位
specify	[ˈspesifai]	vt.	具体指定；详细指明；明确说明
certificate	[səˈtifikit]	n.	凭证，证书，证明书，执照

cement [si'ment]	n.	水泥
binder ['baində]	n.	黏合剂，黏结剂
aggregate ['ægrigit]	n.	（拌水泥用的）粒料，骨料
	vt.	聚集，集合
placement ['pleismənt]	n.	放置，布置
consolidation [kən,sɔli'deiʃən]	n.	巩固，加强，强化
ready-mix ['redi'miks]	a.	掺水即可用的
raw [rɔ:]	a.	未加工的，处于自然状态的；生的
compact [kəm'pækt]	vt.	压紧，（使）坚实，把……紧压在一起
cast [kɑ:st]	vt.	投，扔，抛；浇铸
infinite ['infinit]	a.	无限的，无穷的
contractor [kən'træktə]	n.	承包人，承包商
conversant ['kɔnvəsənt]	a.	熟悉的，精通的
compressive [kəm'presiv]	a.	有压缩力的
shear [ʃiə]	n.	剪切，剪力
tension ['tenʃən]	n.	张力，拉力；拉紧，绷紧
stiffness ['stifnis]	n.	硬挺度，抗挠性
utilize ['ju:tilaiz]	vt.	利用，使用
span [spæn]	vt.	（桥、拱等）横跨，跨越
	n.	跨距；跨度
cable ['keibl]	n.	缆，索，钢索
bloom [blu:m]	n.	繁荣，兴盛，成长，大量出现
runway ['rʌnwei]	n.	（机场的）跑道；（停车场的）车道，通道
tunnel ['tʌnəl]	n.	隧道，地道
pipeline ['paip,lain]	n.	导管，输油管

platform ['plæt,fɔ:m]	n.	平台，台
edible ['edibl]	a.	可食的，食用的
construction material		建筑材料
comply with		按要求、命令去做，依从，顺从，服从
raw material		原材料
above all		首先，尤其是，最重要的是
It follows that		因此，所以，必然是
cable-stayed bridge		斜拉桥
as of now		到目前为止
such that		到这样的程度

Notes

1. Its worldwide production exceeds that of steel by a factor of 10 in tonnage and by more than a factor of 30 in volume.

   全世界混凝土的生产吨位是钢材的 10 倍，体积是钢材的 30 多倍。

   句中 by a factor of 是 "以……倍（增加或减少）" 的意思。

2. 香港国际金融中心（简称国金；英文：International Finance Center，IFC）是香港作为世界级金融中心的著名地标，位于香港岛中环金融街 8 号，面向维多利亚港。由著名美籍建筑师 César Pelli 及香港建筑师严迅奇合作设计而成，总楼面面积达 43.6 万平方米。

Exercises

Ⅰ. Answer the following questions according to the text.

1. Why has concrete become so popular in the world?
2. What are the commonly used structural materials in a concrete structure?
3. Which factors have influence on the quality of cast concrete structure?
4. How are the potential qualities of concrete determined?
5. What are the functions of concrete in a concrete structure?
6. How have concretes been widely used? Please list examples.

7. How do you know the importance of concrete from the passage?

8. Browse the Internet and find out more about concrete.

Ⅱ. Translate the following terms into Chinese.

1. structural material

2. raw materials

3. the potential qualities of concrete

4. compressive force

5. shear force

6. high-strength concrete

7. cable-stayed bridge

8. a high-speed rail system

参考译文

混凝土：一种结构材料

混凝土是世界上使用最广泛的建筑材料，它受欢迎的原因可归结为两个方面：第一，混凝土可用于多种不同的建筑结构，诸如水坝、路面、建筑框架或桥梁，要比其他任何建筑材料用得多；第二，混凝土的使用量超过了其他任何材料。全世界混凝土的生产吨位是钢材的10倍，体积是钢材的30多倍。

在混凝土结构中，混凝土和钢材是两种常用的结构材料。所谓的结构材料是指既能承受自身重量还能承受其他荷载的材料。

钢材通常是在设备尖端的工厂生产的，其生产条件受到严格控制。每一种钢材的特性要在实验室中进行测定，并要在生产商的许可证书上加以描述。因此，钢材结构设计师需依据相关的标准对钢材进行详细说明，建造商要确保钢材的正确使用和钢材与钢材间的恰当连接。

另一方面，混凝土的生产方式较为粗糙，其质量也大相径庭。甚至混凝土黏合剂水泥的质量也由制造商保证，其方法和钢材的类似。尽管如此，由于多种因素，诸如骨料、混合程序，混凝土生产操作者的技巧、存放和坚固性能等的影响，混凝土的质量是很难确保的。

从预拌混凝土供应商手中购买特定质量的混凝土有一定可能，但在这种情况下，这仅仅是买来用于施工的原材料。运输、存放，尤其是压塑，会大大影响现浇混凝土结构的质量。此外，混凝土不像钢材，其混合物的选择实际上没有限制，因此，需对混凝土的特性和性态了如指掌才能作出相应的选择。设计师兼规定者的能力决定混凝土的潜在质量，供应商和承包商的能力控制成品结构中混凝土的实际质量，所以，他们必须精通混凝土的特性、制造和放置方法。

在混凝土结构中，混凝土主要承载挤压力和剪切力，而钢材承担张力。另外，混凝土用来固定建筑物结构以保持其稳固。

各种结构中都在广泛使用混凝土，高强混凝土已被用在许多高层建筑物的建造中。在香港，80 级混凝土（80MPa）被用于浇注最高建筑物的柱子，如图 4.1 所示，这是修建于 2003 年的香港国际金融中心，共 88 层，高 415 米（1362 英尺）。

图 4.1　香港国际金融中心

混凝土也可用于桥梁建设。图 4.2 为最近建造的苏通大桥，横跨长江，连接南通和常熟（江苏省苏州市的卫星市）两市，跨径为 1088 米，是目前世界上跨径最大的斜拉桥，两侧跨径各为 300 米（984 英尺），并有 4 个小斜拉索跨径。

图 4.2　江苏苏州苏通大桥

水坝也是混凝土备受欢迎的另一应用领域。修建于 20 世纪 30 年代的胡弗水坝和库里大水坝是最早的两大混凝土水坝，他们至今仍巍然屹立在那。世界上最大的水坝是我国湖北省的三峡大坝，如图4.3所示。大坝混凝土用量超过了2200万立方米。

图4.3 湖北三峡大坝

混凝土也可用于修建高速铁路。世界上第一条现代化高容量（最初火车车厢多达12节）高铁是1964年日本修建的新干线。1965年6月在欧洲慕尼黑国际交通运输博览会介绍了高铁。如今，我国高铁的修建如火如荼，2013年底，中国高速铁路运营里程达到1.1万公里，居世界首位，已占世界总里程的一半。图4.4为我国高速铁路系统。

图4.4 高速铁路

此外，混凝土还被广泛用于修建机场跑道、隧道、高速公路、管道和石油平台。到目前为止，每年全世界混凝土的消费量达到这样一个数值，如果混凝土可食，地球上的每一个人每年要"吃掉"2000千克。你也许会惊异混凝土为什么这么受欢迎。

Reading Material: Brick Manufacture and Use in Construction

Bricks are blocks of clay that have been hardened through being fired in a kiln or dried in the sun. Over time, kiln-fired bricks have grown more popular than sun-dried bricks, although both are still found worldwide. Bricks have been in continual used for around 5000 years, and brickwork from this time still stands in the Middle East, a testament to its durability.

The Roman Legions first brought bricks to Britain, using mobile kilns to construct roads, aqueduct and buildings across the country. Bricks were especially favored in the 18th and 19th centuries, although their use has declined over the last 50 years due to the increased availability of cement and concrete.

Manufacture of Bricks

In the past, bricks came in many different shapes and sizes, but today's modern bricks tend to be a standard size of around 8″ × 4″ × 2″. They demonstrate a wide variety of textures, colors and finishes from yellows, reds and purples to smooth, rough and rustic. These are due to the mineral variations found in the clay, and the method of manufacturing.

Bricks are traditionally manufactured by mixing clay with enough water to form a mud that is then poured into a mould of the desired shape and size, and hardened through fire or sun. Adobe bricks, very fashionable in parts of the USA, are still made in this way with a mixture of clay and sand(and sometimes manure and straw)being poured into a form, and then removed and dried in stacks outside in the sun.

Compressed Earth Blocks (CEBs) were developed in the 1950s and are similar to adobe bricks, except they are more compact and uniform. They are manufactured from soil that is more sand than clay, and compressed using a manual or motorized machine to produce a variety of block shapes, including hollow designs for insulation. CEBs are highly energy efficient using up to 15 times less energy than a fired brick. They are durable, ecological, inexpensive, and utilize low technology. For this reason they are increasingly used in developing countries as a sustainable building technology.

Modern methods of brick manufacture are highly mechanized and automated procedures whereby clay are extruded in a continuous column, wirecut into bricks, and hydraulically pressed to ensure resistance to weathering. The bricks are then dried and slow fired at around 1000℃ ~ 1200℃. In more recent times, recycled glass and other waste materials have been introduced into this process. These materials have been found to reduce firing times, temperatures and toxic emissions, improve brick strength and durability, and reduce waste going to landfill.

Brick Laying

Bricks are laid flat in rows called courses, exposing either their sides (stretcher) or ends (header). The pattern of overlap created by the course is called a bond. There are several different kinds of bonds, including Stretcher (most common), Herringbone, English, Basket and Flemish. With all bonds, the vertical joints between each course of bricks must not line up or the structure will be weakened.

Bricks are usually held together by mortar, though some bricks such as CEBs can be dry stacked. Mortar consists of sand, a binding agent (traditionally lime but these days more often cement) and water, which is then mixed to a thick paste. It is applied to a brick, which is then placed onto another brick and allowed to dry. Pointing refers to the visible edge of the mortar between the bricks, which is finished with a special trowel to provide a decorative look to the brickwork.

When building a structure, a bed of mortar is laid on the top of the foundation, and the structure's ends are built up first. A string is then stretched between these ends to ensure each row of bricks stays level. Two layers of brick are used to create a stronger structure, with a gap left for insulation purposes. A wide range of structures including arches can be built using bricks.

Bricks as a Sustainable Building Material

Bricks are a versatile and durable building and construction material, with good load-bearing properties, high thermal mass and potential low energy impact. In the case of simple earth bricks such as adobe and CEBs, they measure high on the sustainability index, being made from locally available (and abundant) materials of clay, sand, and water, using low technology compression equipment, solar energy or kilns. While modern methods of brick construction have a much lower sustainability index, the UK brick industry has developed a strategy to minimize its environmental impact and increase its energy efficiency and use of renewable energies. Overall, bricks are a good example of a sustainable building practice and are currently gaining in popularity around the world.

New Words and Expressions

clay [kleɪ]   n.   黏土，泥土
kiln [kɪln]   n.   （用来烧或烘干砖等的）窑，炉

Building Materials Unit 4

brickwork ['brikwəːk]	n.	砌砖
testament ['testəmənt]	n.	证明，证据
durability [ˌdjurə'biliti]	n.	耐久性，耐用性
legion ['liːdʒən]	n.	古罗马军团
aqueduct ['ækwiˌdʌkt]	n.	高架渠；导水管；渡槽
texture ['tekstʃə]	n.	（材料等的）构造；（岩石等的）纹理
rustic ['rʌstik]	a.	粗面石工的；用粗糙的木材或树枝制作的
mould [məuld]	n.	铸模，模型
	vt.	用模子做，浇铸
mineral ['minərəl]	n. & a.	矿物；矿石；矿物质；矿物的，矿质的
adobe [ə'dəubi]	n.	砖坯，土砖
stack [stæk]	n.	堆，垛，大量，一大堆
	vt. & vi.	堆积
uniform ['juːnifɔːm]	a.	全都相同的，一律的，清一色的
manual ['mænjuəl]	a.	用手的，手工的
motorize ['məutəraiz]	vt.	使机动化
hollow ['hɔləu]	a.	凹陷的；空的；中空的
insulation [ˌinsə'leiʃən]	n.	隔离，隔绝；绝缘；隔热
ecological [ˌekə'lɔdʒikəl]	a.	生态的；生态学的
sustainable [sə'steinəbl]	a.	可持续的
mechanize ['mekənaiz]	vt. & vi.	使（过程、工厂等）机械化
automate ['ɔːtəmeit]	vt. & vi.	（使）自动化
extrude [eks'truːd]	v.	挤压出，挤压成；突出，伸出；逐出
hydraulically [hai'drɔːlikəli]	ad.	通过水（或液）压

weather	['weðə]	v.	晒干；风化
toxic	['tɔksik]	a.	有毒的；中毒的
emission	[i'miʃən]	n.	排放(物)
overlap	[ˌəuvə'læp]	n.	重叠的部分
		vt. & vi.	部分重叠
bond	[bɔnd]	n.	黏结；黏合；契约
stretcher	['stretʃə]	n.	顺砌砖；横砌石
herringbone	['heriŋbəun]	n.	鲱鱼鱼骨，交叉缝式，人字形
joint	[dʒɔint]	n.	接头，接缝；接合点
		a.	共同的，联合的
agent	['eidʒənt]	n.	作用剂；作用者，原动力，动因
lime	[laim]	n.	石灰
trowel	['trauəl]	n.	泥刀，抹子，小铲子
string	[striŋ]	n.	线，细绳
layer	['leiə]	n.	层，层次
arch	[a:tʃ]	n.	拱，拱门
versatile	['və:sətail]	a.	(指工具、机器等)多用途的，多功能的
thermal	['θə:məl]	a	热的，热量的，由热造成的
index	['indeks]	n.	指数，指标；索引，卡片索引，文献索引
compression	[kəm'preʃən]	a.	挤压，压缩
solar	['səulə]	a.	太阳的，日光的
strategy	['strætidʒi]	n.	战略，策略
renewable	[ri'njuəbl]	a.	可更新的，可恢复的，可继续的
in use			在使用中
up to			(数量上)多达
in the case of			至于……，就……来说；就……而论

Unit 5

Construction Surveying

Text: What "Construction Surveying" is About

"To construct" means "to built" or "to put together". The purpose of construction surveying is to carry out surveying measurements required for the realization of a construction on a site. Such a construction might be a road, a school, a canal, a storage dam, or the like. What has to be "surveyed" and how the required measurements must be accomplished depend on both the construction and the site.

A site cannot be described geometrically by means of a site map alone. A map describes a site geometrically, but in a horizontal sense only. In many cases, a site needs also to be described geometrically in a vertical sense. This is enabled via so-called "sections" (Fig. 5.1 and Fig. 5.2).

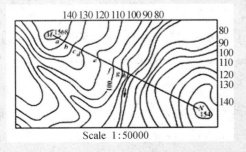

Fig. 5.1 Site Map

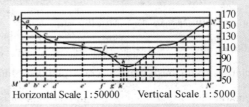

Fig. 5.2 Sectional View

Surveying Procedures

When it comes to surveying activities within the framework of realizing a construction, three steps must be clearly discerned.

Firstly, preparing for the construction involves horizontal and vertical geometric description by means of surveying measurements. This procedure is generally called "mapping" because the description is often provided by way of a site map. The initial result of a site survey, however, is a field sketch, not yet a site map.

Secondly, a site map has to be produced from the field sketch. A site map provides the basis for designing the layout of a construction with respect to the site. However, if dimensions are actually to be determined during and not in advance of construction, then the intermediate step of a site map is not needed.

Finally, a construction layout is always to be set out on the site with its true dimensions and in the right position. The procedure called "setting out" is also known as "staking out". It requires the same measurement techniques as used for mapping a site.

Construction Methods

Man-made constructions have been successfully built all over the world for millennia. Examples are bridges, irrigation systems, bench terraces, dams for water retention and kinds of buildings. Though in a distant past surveying measurements were not required to build them, such structures still needed to be properly dimensioned. This could be achieved by following a construction method best described as "dimensioned during construction". However, when a construction is to be realized according to some design, then "built as designed" is the construction method to be followed.

Surveying measurements are required to properly set out the designed layout. The Great Pyramids in Egypt shown in Fig. 5.3 were constructed "as designed" several millennia ago. Extinct Indian cultures in the Middle and South Americas realized impressive constructions also. By modern standards the surveying techniques applied here were very simple, despite the size and complexity of these historic constructions. Simplicity of surveying technology also characterized the construction techniques of the industrious Romans. A great number of their constructions still stand all over Southern Europe, the Middle East and North Africa (Fig. 5.4).

Fig. 5.3 Pyramids in Egypt

Fig. 5.4 the Colosseum of Rome

Drawing or Sketching a Planned Construction

A map implicitly reveals dimensions, because dimensions are contained in the graph itself. These are the signs on a map referring to real world dimensions shown in Fig. 5.5.

- a numerical scale ratio (for instance 1∶500)
- a graphical scale bar
- a grid of evenly spaced squares

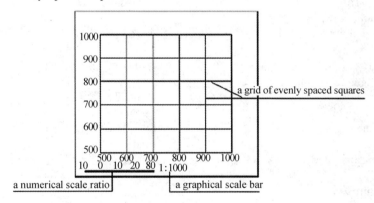

Fig. 5.5 A Numerical Scale Ratio, A Graphical Scale Bar, A Grid of Evenly Spaced Squares

This is different from a construction drawing. In a construction drawing, all relevant measures and dimensions must be explicitly registered in numerical form.

The reason why a construction drawing explicitly and numerically provides all relevant dimensions is for reliability, because the drawing will be used in building the construction. Parts of the construction will be fabricated separately. When assembled on site, all parts must fit. Dimensional accuracy needs to be a few centimeters, or even millimeters. It would be very difficult to achieve this accuracy if trying to derive dimensions of parts by calculation from measurements on a drawing made using an ordinary ruler. This would not only be inconvenient and cumbersome, but more importantly, unreliable. The use of a ruler is too crude. Deriving dimensions in this way is prone to errors, both in the measurements themselves and in the calculation of the true dimensions drawn from them.

New Words and Expressions

construct	[kən'strʌkt]	vt.	建筑；建造；构成；形成
survey	[sə'vei]	vt.	测量；调查；观察
measurement	['meʒəmənt]	n.	衡量，测量；尺寸，大小
site	[sait]	n.	地点，位置；工地
canal	[kə'næl]	n.	运河；沟渠
dam	[dæm]	n.	水坝，堤，水闸
geometric	[dʒiə'metrik]	a.	几何学的，图形的
geometrically	[dʒiə'metrikəli]	ad.	按几何学原理；按几何图形
horizontal	[hɔri'zɔntl]	a.	平的；水平的；地平的
vertical	['vəːtikəl]	a.	垂直的，竖的，直立的
section	['sekʃən]	n.	断面；剖面；断面图；拆；段；部分
procedure	[prə'siːdʒə]	n.	步骤；程序；工艺规程，生产过程
framework	['freimwəːk]	n.	骨架；构架工程；结构；框架
mapping	['mæpiŋ]	n.	绘制地图，制图，绘图
sketch	[sketʃ]	n.	简图，草图
layout	['leiaut]	n.	布局；计划；设计；方案
dimension	[di'menʃən]	n.	方面，特点；尺寸，大小；体积；范围
distant	['distənt]	a.	（空间或时间）遥远的，远隔的
pyramid	['pirəmid]	n.	金字塔；椎体
standard	['stændəd]	n.	标准，水准；规范，规格

graph	[græf]	n.	图，图表，曲线图
graphical	['græfikəl]	a.	图解的；绘图的；生动的
sign	[sain]	n.	标记，符号；标志；迹象
numerical	[njuː'merikəl]	n.	数字的，用数字表示的，数值的
scale	[skeil]	n.	规模；等级；刻度，标度；比例尺
ratio	['reiʃiəu]	n.	比，比率
grid	[grid]	n.	栅格，网格；地图的坐标方格；输电网
evenly	['iːvənli]	ad.	均匀地；平坦地；平和地
square	[skwɛə]	n.	正方形
accuracy	['ækjurəsi]	n.	正确性，准确，精度，准确度；精密性
cumbersome	['kʌmbəsəm]	a.	笨重的；迟缓而缺乏效率的
prone	[prəun]	a.	易于……的；很可能……的；有……倾向的
scope	[skəup]	n.	范围；余地，机会
illustrate	['iləstreit]	vt.	说明，图解，举例说明
envisage	[in'vizidʒ]	vt.	想象，设想
depend on			依赖，依靠；取决于，随……而定
by means of			用某办法；借助于某事物
when it comes to			当涉及；当谈到
by way of			经过，经由；通过……的方法
with respect to			涉及，提到或关于某事物；在……方面
in advance of			提前；提早；预先；事先；在……之前
prone to			易于某事物；很可能做某事
bench terrace			水平梯田

Notes

1. What has to be "surveyed" and how the required measurements must be accomplished depend on both the construction and the site.

   测量内容以及测量方法则取决于建筑物和建设场地两个方面。

   句中 What has to be "surveyed" 指测量内容。

2. preparing for the construction involves horizontal and vertical geometric description by means of surveying measurements.

   施工的准备工作涉及利用测量数据所进行的平面和高程意义上的几何描述。

   by means of：用某办法；借助于某事物。

3. Extinct Indian cultures in the Middle and South Americas realized impressive constructions also.

   已消亡的中美洲和南美洲的印第安文化中也有这样不凡的建筑。

   cultures：此处为可数名词，特指体现在文艺等方面的智力表现的形式，如 She has studied the cultures of Oriental countries. 她研究过东方各国的文化。

4. The reason why a construction drawing explicitly and numerically provides all relevant dimensions is for reliability, because the drawing will be used in building the construction.

   施工图之所以要清楚地以数字标示所有相关的尺寸在于它的可靠性，因为在建筑施工过程中要用施工图。

Exercises

Ⅰ. Answer the following questions according to the text.

1. What is the purpose of construction surveying?

2. According to the article, in what way should a site be described?

3. What does it involve when preparing for the construction?

4. In the distant past, what method was to be followed in order to dimension a structure?

5. When a construction is to be realized according to some design, what construction method is to be followed?

6. What are the signs used in a map referring to a real world dimensions?

7. What is the difference between a site map and a construction drawing?

8. Why a construction drawing should provides all relevant dimensions explicitly and numerically?

9. Is it good to use ordinary rulers in construction surveying in order to achieve accuracy? Why?

Ⅱ. Translate the following terms into Chinese.

1. construction surveying
2. site map
3. field sketch
4. construction layout
5. setting out
6. staking out
7. bench terrace
8. construction drawing

参考译文

什么是"施工测量"

"施工"意为"建造"或"构筑"。施工测量的目的是应工地工程施工的需要而进行测量,标志出具体位置。建设对象可能是公路、学校、运河、蓄水坝等。测量内容以及测量方法则取决于建筑物和建设场地两个方面。

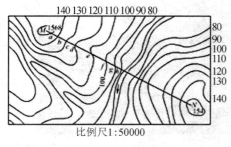

图 5.1　平面图

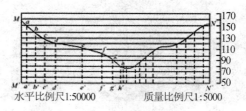

图 5.2　断面图

施工场地不能只用施工平面图进行几何描述。施工平面图能对施工场地进行几何描述,但这种描述只是平面意义的。在许多情况下,也需要对施工场地进行高程上的几何描述,这可以通过"断面图"来实现,如图 5.1 和图 5.2 所示。

测量流程

当涉及工程施工的测量时,必须要搞清楚 3 个步骤。

首先,施工的准备工作涉及利用测量数据所进行的平面和高程意义上的几何描述。这一步骤一般称做"制图"，因为这种描述通常是通过施工图来实现的。但施工场地测量的最初结果只是一个地形图，并非施工图。

其次，施工图必须根据地形图进行绘制。地形图为工地的施工布局提供设计基础。然而，如果尺寸大小实际上是在施工过程中而不是提前确定的，工地图的中间步骤也就可以省去了。

最后，施工布局通常要根据其实际尺寸和正确的位置标定在实地。这一过程叫做"放线"，又叫"放样"。它需要用与测绘工地相同的测量技术。

工程施工方法

几千年来，人工建筑物已经成功地建造于世界各地，如桥梁、水利灌溉设施、水平梯田、蓄水坝和各种建筑物等。虽然在古代，兴修此类建筑并不需要测量数据，但这些建筑结构也需要合理的尺寸。这种施工用的是一种叫做"边建边量"的方法。但如果要根据设计来进行施工，就要采用"按设计施工"的建造方法。

测量数据要能正确地反映设计布局。几千年前的埃及金字塔就是"按设计"修建的，如图5.3所示。已消亡的中美洲和南美洲的印第安文化中也有这样不凡的建筑。按照现代标准，这些历史建筑虽然规模宏大、机构复杂，但所使用的测量技术是很简单的。勤劳的罗马人的施工技术也是以测量技术简单为特点的。而他们的许多历史建筑仍旧屹立在南欧、中东和北非，如图5.4所示。

图5.3　埃及金字塔

图5.4　罗马斗兽场

为拟规划建筑绘制底图

一张图间接地显示尺寸，因为尺寸包含在图表中。在绘图中这些标记标示了建筑物的实际尺寸，如图5.5所示。

- 数字比例尺（如1∶500）
- 图示比例尺
- 等距方格网

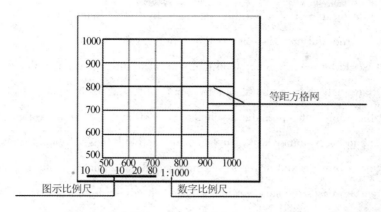

图 5.5 数字比例尺、图示比例尺、等距方格网

这个不同于施工图。施工图必须清楚地用数字标出相关的尺寸大小。

施工图之所以要清楚地以数字标示所有相关的尺寸大小在于它的可靠性,因为在建筑施工过程中要用施工图。建筑物的各个部分将被逐个修建,在施工现场被组合为整体结构时,所有部分必须匹配。尺寸精度要求是几厘米甚至是几毫米。如果试图从用普通的刻度尺绘制的图表计算得出各部分的尺寸,就很难达到要求的精度,这不仅不便计算和累赘,而且更为重要的是缺乏可信度。使用标尺太过粗略,用这种方法所得到的尺寸大小往往会有差错,而测量数据和真实尺寸的计算都来源于此。

Reading Material: The Purpose of the Survey

There are several conditions under which a surveyor may be required to survey or examine a building and the first point to ascertain is the reason for which the advice is being sought. The following is a list of the most usual reasons.

● To prepare a measured drawing of the building to enable a scheme for alterations, improvements or extensions to be prepared.

● To prepare a report on the condition of a property to be purchased.

● To prepare a schedule of condition for a property to be taken on long lease.

● To advise on the repair and preservation of a building (including "listed" buildings).

● Work to be carried out to satisfy the requirements of the local or other authority, i.e. dangerous structure notices, public health notices or a factory inspector's notice.

● To prepare plans in connection with party wall agreements. This is usually required where alterations to a party wall are contemplated.

- To advise on the repair of a building damaged by fire or flood.
- To make a structural appraisal of existing buildings for "change of use".

No doubt it would be readily understood that several of the surveys mentioned above would be carried out simultaneously. For instance, a surveyor is often asked to report on the condition of a property and at the same time prepare a scheme for an extension or alterations. The surveyor's report on the items to be examined will also vary with each building; a lot will depend on whether or not the surveyor is being asked to report on the general condition of a building or examine specific defects. In certain cases the surveyor may consider it advisable to ask if there is any particular point which the client has noticed and which might be giving them reason for concern. Initially, the client will almost certainly be worried by the question of structural stability and will wish to have the surveyor's advice on this matter as soon as possible. On accepting instructions, the surveyor must therefore arrange an early date to examine the premises with this object in mind. Owners seldom realise that a building ten or more years of age is unlikely to be in perfect condition; even in quite small properties expenditure may have to be incurred in order to put the property in sound condition.

Reference to the early history of the building is often important. Very few owners can provide clear details about old buildings. Local authorities or local builders can often produce the original plans, but it is well to remember that alterations were often carried out in the past without submitting plans to the authorities concerned, so any drawings produced should be checked carefully. It was also quite common for details to be altered at the time of building but not amended on the plans.

New Words and Expressions

ascertain [æsə'tein]	vt.	查明；弄清；确定
list [list]	n.	一览表；清单
extension [ik'stenʃən]	n.	伸长；延长；延展，伸展；增加；扩大
property ['prɔpəti]	n.	财产；资产；特性，性能，属性
purchase ['pəːtʃəs]	vt. & n.	买，购买
schedule ['skedʒul]	n.	进度表；预定计划表；清单，明细表

lease	[liːs]	n.	租约，租契
local	[ˈləukəl]	a.	地方的；本地的
authority	[ɔːˈθɔriti]	n.	权力；权威；当局，官方；管理机构
inspector	[inˈspektə]	n.	检查员；视察员；巡视员；检验员
contemplate	[ˈkɔntempleit]	vt.	盘算，计议；周密考虑
appraisal	[əˈpreizəl]	n.	估计，估量；评价；鉴定
simultaneously	[saiməlˈteiniəsli]	ad.	同时，一起
item	[ˈaitəm]	n.	条款，节；名称；物品，零件，设备
vary	[ˈvɛəri]	vi.	改变，变动，变化
specific	[spiˈsifik]	a.	特定的；具体的；确切的
defect	[diˈfekt]	n.	缺点；不足之处；毛病；瑕疵
advisable	[ədˈvaizəbl]	a.	可取；明智
particular	[pəˈtikjulə]	a.	个别的；特别的；特殊的
		n.	信息；细节；事项
point	[pɔint]	n.	点；尖端；要点；目标；分数；特点
client	[ˈklaiənt]	n.	建设单位；委托人；买主，顾客
initially	[iˈniʃəli]	ad.	最初，开始
stability	[stəˈbiliti]	n.	稳定；稳定性，稳定度
instruction	[inˈstrʌkʃən]	n.	用法说明，操作指南；吩咐，命令
arrange	[əˈreindʒ]	n.	安排；准备，筹划；整理；布置
premises	[ˈpremisiz]	n.	（包括附属建筑、土地等在内的）房屋或其他建筑物
incur	[inˈkə]	vt.	遭受；蒙受；招致；引起；带来
sound	[saund]	a.	完好的；健康的；健全的；无损伤的
original	[əˈridʒənəl]	a.	原始的；最初的；原先的

submit	[səb'mit]	vt.	呈送，提交
alter	['ɔːltə]	vt. & vi	改变；更改，变更；修改
commission	[kə'miʃən]	n.	任务；委托
amend	[ə'mend]	vt.	改正；改善；改进
propose	[prə'pəuz]	vt.	提议；提名，推荐；打算，计划
commence	[kə'mens]	vt.	开始
agreement	[ə'griːmənt]	n.	契约，合同，协议，一致；符合
reposition	[riːpə'ziʃən]	vt.	调换位置
essential	[i'senʃəl]	a.	必要的；不可缺少的
adjoining	[ə'dʒɔiniŋ]	a.	毗邻的，邻接的；伴随的
rear	[riə]	n.	后部；后面；背后
drainage	['dreinidʒ]	n.	排水；排水设备
omission	[əu'miʃən]	n.	遗漏；省略
clause	[klɔːz]	n.	条款
termination	[təːmi'neiʃən]	n.	终点；结局；终止
dispute	[dis'pjuːt]	n. & vi.	争论，争端
identify	[ai'dentifai]	vt.	识别，等同，标志
attach	[ə'tætʃ]	vt.	附着，附属
investigate	[in'vestigeit]	vt.	调查，调查研究
bulge	[bʌldʒ]	vi.	鼓起；凸出
settlement	['setlmənt]	n.	沉陷；沉积物；沉淀，下沉，沉积
entirely	[in'taiəli]	ad.	完全地；彻底地
plumb	[plʌm]	vt.	用铅垂线测
party wall			界墙；共用墙
tell-tale			位移指示器
listed building			注册的文物保护建筑物

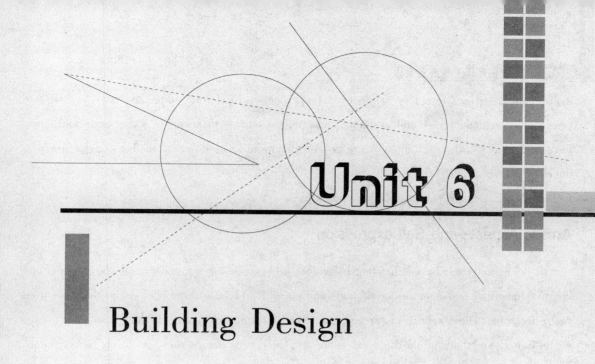

Unit 6

Building Design

Text: One of the Architectural Design Values—Aesthetic Design Values

The expansion of architectural and industrial design ideas and vocabularies which took place during the 20th century has created a diverse aesthetic reality within these two domains. This pluralistic and diverse aesthetic reality has typically been created within different architectural and industrial design movements such as: Modernism, Postmodernism, Deconstructivism, Poststructuralism, Neoclassicism, New Expressionism, Supermodernism etc. All of these aesthetic realities represent a number of divergent aesthetic values, in addition to differences in general values and theories found within these movements. Some of the stylistic distinctions found in these diverse aesthetic realities reflect profound differences in design values and thinking, but this is not the case for all stylistic distinctions, as some stylistic distinctions builds on similar thinking and values.

These aesthetic values and their diverse aesthetic expressions are to some degree a reflection of the development that has taken place in the art community. In addition, these diverse aesthetic expressions are also a reflection of individual architects and industrial designers' personal expression, based on designers' tendency to experiment with form, materials, and ornament to create new aesthetic styles and aesthetic vocabulary. Changes in aesthetic styles and expressions have been, and still are, both synchronic and diachronic, as different aesthetic styles are produced and promoted simultaneously.

Aesthetic Design Values contain seven values.

Artistic Aspects and Self-expression

It is characterized by a belief that individual self-expression—or one's inner spiritual self and creative imagination, inner resources and intuition—should be utilized and/or be the base used when designing. These sentiments are closely linked to a number of artistic values found in movements like Expressionism and the avant-garde art. Thus, this design value is closely related to abstract forms and expression, personal creative liberty, elitism and being ahead of the rest of society.

The Spirit of the Times Design Value

This design value is based on the conception that every age has a certain spirit or set of shared attitudes that should be utilized when designing. The spirit of the times denotes the intellectual and cultural climate of a particular era, which can be linked to an experience of a certain worldview, sense of taste, collective consciousness and unconsciousness. Thus "form expression" which can be found, to some extent in the "air" of a given time and each generation, should generate an aesthetic style that expresses the uniqueness related to that time.

The Structural, Functional and Material Honesty Design Value

Structural honesty is linked to the notion that a structure shall display its "true" purpose and not be decorative etc. Functional honesty is linked to the idea that a building or product form shall be shaped on the basis of its intended function, often known as "form follows function". Material honesty implies that materials should be used and selected on the bases of their properties, and that the characteristics of a material should influence the form it is used for. Thus, a material must not be used as a substitute for another material as this subverts the materials' "true" properties and it is "cheating" the spectator.

The Simplicity and Minimalism Design Value

This design value is based on the idea that simple forms, i.e. aesthetics without considerable ornaments, simple geometry, smooth surfaces etc., represents forms which are both truer to "real" art and represents "folk" wisdom. This design value implies that the more cultivated a person becomes, the more decoration disappears. In addition, it is linked to the notion that simple forms will free people from the everyday clutter, thus contribute to tranquility and restfulness.

The Nature and Organic Design Value

This design value is based on the idea that nature (i.e. all sorts of living organisms, numerical laws etc.) can provide inspiration, functional clues and aesthetic forms that architects and industrial designers should use as a basis for designs. Designs based on this value tend to be characterized by free-flowing curves, asymmetrical lines and expressive forms. This design value can be summed up in "form follows flow" or "of the hill" as oppose to "on the hill".

The Classic, Traditional and Vernacular Aesthetics Design Value

This value is based on a belief that a building and product should be designed from timeless principles that transcend particular designers, cultures and climates. Implicit in this design value is the notion that if these forms are used, the public will appreciate a structure's timeless beauty and understand immediately how to use a given building or product. This design value is also linked to regional differences i.e. varying climate etc. and folklore cultures, which creates distinctive aesthetical expressions.

The Regionalism Design Value

This design value is based on the belief that building—and to some degree products—should be designed in accordance with the particular characteristics of a specific place. In addition, it is linked to the aim of achieving visual harmony between a building and its surroundings, as well as achieving continuity in a given area. In other words, it strives to create a connection between past and present forms of building. Finally, this value is also often related to preserving and creating regional and national identity.

New Words and Expressions

architectural	[ˌɑːkiˈtektʃərəl]	a.	建筑上的，建筑学的
aesthetic	[iːsˈθetik]	a.	有关美的，美学的；审美的；悦目的，雅致的
diverse	[daiˈvəːs]	a.	不同的；多种多样的
domain	[dəuˈmein]	n.	范围，领域
pluralistic	[ˌpluərəˈlistik]	a.	多元的；兼职的，兼任的
divergent	[daiˈvəːdʒənt]	a.	有分歧的；叉开的
stylistic	[staiˈlistik]	a.	风格上的
distinction	[disˈtiŋkʃən]	a.	区别，明显差别，特征
thinking	[ˈθiŋkiŋ]	n.	思想，思考；想法；意见；见解
tendency	[ˈtendənsi]	n.	倾向，趋势
ornament	[ˈɔːnəmənt]	n.	装饰，点缀；装饰品，点缀品
synchronic	[siŋˈkrɔnik]	a.	同时期的，同时发生的
diachronic	[daiəˈkrɔnik]	a.	历时的
characterize	[ˈkæriktəraiz]	vt.	是……的特征，以……为特征
contemporary	[kənˈtempərəri]	a.	当代的；同时代的，同属一个时期的
inner	[ˈinə]	a.	内部的，里面的
intuition	[ˌintjuˈiʃən]	n.	直觉
sentiment	[ˈsentimənt]	n.	温情；伤感；观点，主意
avant-garde	[ˌævˈgɑːd]	n.	革新者，艺术上的先锋派
elitism	[eiˈliːtizm]	n.	精英主义；精英意识
shared	[ʃɛəd]	a.	共享的，共用的
denote	[diˈnəut]	vt.	指示，指出

collective [kə'lektiv]		a.	集体的，共同的，共有的
generate ['dʒenəreit]		vt.	生成，产生；引起，导致
substitute ['sʌbstitjuːt]		n.	代用品，代替者，代替物
		vt. & vi.	代替，替换，代用
subvert [sʌb'vəːt]		vt.	颠覆，破坏（政治制度、宗教信仰等）
spectator ['spekteitə]		n.	观众，旁观者
geometry [dʒi'ɔmitri]		n.	几何（学）
tranquility [træŋ'kwiliti]		n.	宁静
organism ['ɔːgənizəm]		n.	有机物，有机体；生物；有机体系
curve [kəːv]		n.	曲线，弧线
asymmetrical [ˌeisi'metrikl]		a.	不均匀的，不对称的
transcend [træn'send]		vt.	超出或超越
implicit [im'plisit]		a.	不言明的，含蓄的
folklore ['fəuklɔː]		n.	民间传统；民间故事；民俗
distinctive [dis'tiŋktiv]		a.	有特色的，与众不同的
regionalism ['riːdʒənəˌlizəm]		n.	地方主义，乡土主义，乡土色彩
in addition to			加之，除……之外
to some degree			在某种程度上
be based on			以……为基础，根据
as well as			也，又
in accordance with			与……一致，依照

Notes

1. ... different architectural and industrial design movements such as: Modernism, Postmodernism, Deconstructivism, Post-structuralism, Neoclassicism, New Expressionism, Supermod-

ernism etc.

这句话提到了建筑和工业设计的各个流派：现代主义，后现代主义，解构主义，后解构主义，新古典主义，新表现主义和超现代主义等，不同的流派对建筑设计产生了深远的影响。

2. ... but this is not the case for all stylistic distinctions, as some stylistic distinctions builds on similar thinking and values.

句中 as 引导原因状语从句，通常置于句首。

3. ... based on designers' tendency to experiment with form, materials, and ornament to create new aesthetic styles and aesthetic vocabulary.

to experiment with form, materials, and ornament 作后置定语，修饰 tendency，to create new aesthetic styles and aesthetic vocabulary 作目的状语，to 相当于 in order to。

Exercises

Ⅰ. Answer the following questions according to the text.

1. How has a diverse aesthetic reality been created?
2. What do aesthetic realities represent within these architectural and industrial design movements?
3. What do aesthetic values and their aesthetic expressions reflect?
4. How do you understand the spirit of the time design value?
5. What does "form follows flow" mean?
6. What does the regionalism design value imply?
7. How do you apply these values to architectural design?
8. Please browse the internet, have an understanding of architectural design movements.

Ⅱ. Translate the following terms into Chinese.

1. aesthetic reality
2. architectural and industrial design movements
3. aesthetic expression
4. individual self-expression
5. avant-garde art
6. collective consciousness
7. a structure's timeless beauty
8. visual harmony between a building and its surroundings

参考译文

建筑设计观之美学设计观

20世纪，建筑和工业设计理念的提高及词汇的丰富在这两个领域已创造了一个丰富多样的美学现实。这种多元化的美学现实在不同的建筑和工业设计运动，如现代主义、后现代主义、解构主义、后结构主义、新古典主义、新表现主义、超现代主义等中已被典型地创造出来。所有这些美学现实体现了诸多相异的美学观和差异，这些差异表现在上述运动的总体理念和理论中。多样的美学现实中的一些风格差异反映了设计观和设计思想的截然不同，但是，对于所有的风格情况并非如此，因为一些风格差异是以相似的思想和价值观为基础的。

此类美学观及其审美表现在某种程度上是艺术领域发展的一种反映。另外，这些多样的审美表现也是建筑师和工业设计师自我表达的一种反映，这种自我表达以设计师的倾向性为基础，即他们倾向于尝试各种形式、材料和装饰以创造新的审美风格和美学词汇。由于不同审美风格的产生和提升是同时发生的，所以审美风格和审美表达的变化一直是共时和历时的。

美学设计观有以下7种。

艺术层面和自我表现

这种价值观的特征是人们坚信应该利用个体的自我表现或者内在精神的自我、创造性想象、内在资源和直觉力，并/或者在设计时以此为基础。这些观点与表现主义、先锋派等运动中倡导的众多艺术观紧密相连，因此，这种设计观与抽象形式、表现方式、个人创作自由、精英意识及社会中其他超前的东西密不可分。

时代精神设计观

这种设计观以此观念为基础，即每个时代都有可用于设计的特定精神和一系列共同看法。时代精神为特定时期的思想和文化风气，与一定的世界观、品味、集体意识和潜意识相连。因此，在某种程度上，在某个特定时代氛围中和每代人身上所体现的"形式表达"应该表现一种与时俱进的独一无二的审美风格。

结构、功能和材料真实性设计观

结构真实性与此理念相联系，即结构应体现其真实的目的而不是装饰等。功能真实性连接的理念是建筑物或产品形式的构造应以原有的功能为基础，这通常称之为"形式随功能"。材料真实性意味着材料的使用和选择应该以其特性为基础，材料的特征应影响其所用于构建的形式，因此，某一种材料绝不能替代其他材料，因为这样会破坏材料的真实特性，并会欺骗旁观者。

极简派艺术设计观

这种设计观认为简洁的形式，即没有大量装饰的美学要素、简单的几何形体、光滑的表面等所代表的形式更接近于"真正"的艺术，也能体现"民众"的智慧。这种设计观暗示了一个人越有教养，装饰就越少。此外，这种设计观还认为简洁的形式会使人远离喧闹，归于宁静。

自然有机的设计观

这种设计观的思想基础是自然(所有生物有机体和用数字表示的法则等)能为建筑师和工业设计家提供用于设计基础的灵感、功能线索和审美形式，基于这种观念的设计常以灵动的曲线、不对称的线条和表现形式为特征。这种设计观可概括为"如水随形"或"融为一体"而非"脱离整体"。

古典、传统及民间风格设计观

这种设计观的基础是人们坚信建筑和产品的设计应不受时间影响，可超越特定的设计师、文化和风气。在这种设计观中隐含着这样的理念，即如果这些形式被采用，公众会欣赏到结构永不衰退的美并迅速懂得如何运用既定的建筑或产品。这种设计观也与创造独特审美表达的地域差异(如不同的气候条件等)和民间文化相联系。

本土设计

这种设计观的基础是建筑和产品应当因地制宜地设计。此外，这种设计观也要达到建筑与周围环境的视觉和谐及取得特定区域的延续性的目的。换句话说，这种设计观在努力创造建筑物过去和现在形式上的关联性。最后，这种设计观也常与地区和民族身份的保留及创造相连。

Reading Material: Model Types

Models are referred to in a variety of ways, and terms may be used interchangeably in different settings. Although there is no standard, the definitions in the following lists are commonly used. All of the model types discussed (sketch, massing, development, etc.) are considered to be study models, including those used for formal presentations. As such, their purpose is to generate design ideas and serve as vehicles for refinement. They can range from quick, rough constructions to resolved models. Whatever state they are in, the term study model implies that they are always open to investigation and refinement.

Study models can be considered to belong to two different groups: primary models and secondary models. The primary set has to do with the level or stage of design evolution, and the secondary set refers to particular sections or aspects of the project under focus. A secondary model may be built as a primary model type, depending on the level of focus. For example, a model used to develop interior spaces would be thought of as an interior model but would also be a sketch model, development model, or presentation model, depending on its level of focus.

Primary Models

Primary models are abstract in concept and are employed to explore different stages of focus.
Sketch
Diagram
Concept
Massing
Solid/Void
Development
Presentation/Finish

Secondary Models

Secondary models are used for particular building or site components.
Site Contour
Site Context/Urban
Entourage/Site Foliage

Interior

Section

Facade

Framing/Structure

Detail/Connections

Sketch Models

Sketch models constitute the initial phase of study models. They are like three-dimensional drawing and sketching—a medium for speed and spontaneity. Sketch models generally are not overly concerned with craft but with providing a quick way to visualize space. They are intended to be cut into and modified as exploration proceeds. These models may also be produced as a quick series to explore variations in a general design direction. Although many of the models shown throughout the book are produced as expressive explorations, sketch models are also valuable when built with greater precision and used to explore qualities of alignment, proportion, and spatial definition.

Sketch models are generally built at relatively small scales from inexpensive materials such as chipboard or poster board.

Several examples of sketch models are shown (Fig. 6. 1 and Fig. 6. 2), ranging from small building propositions to ideas of space and site relationships.

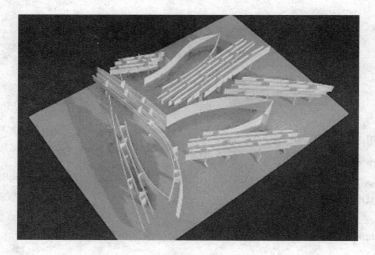

Fig. 6. 1　Sketch Model Ⅰ

Small sketches can be made early in the design phase to explore basic building organizations and reflect general relationships of program circulation and architectural concerns.

Fig. 6. 2 Sketch Model II

Sketch models can explore the 3D relationship between overlapping spaces.

Site Contour Models

Site models, or contour models, are built to study topography and the building's relationship to the site. They typically reproduce the slope of the land, or grade, by employing a series of scaled layers that represent increments of rise and fall in the landscape, as shown in Fig. 6. 3.

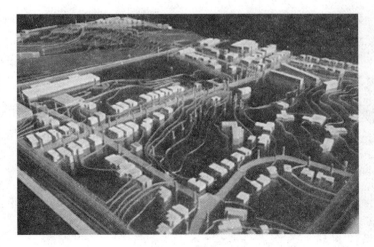

Fig. 6. 3 Site Contour I

As study constructions, they can be modified to fit the building to the site, control water, and implement landscape design.

A typical contour model displays site grades at regular intervals, as shown in Fig. 6.4. Grade increments may represent anywhere from 6″ to 5ft., depending on the size of the site and the size of the model.

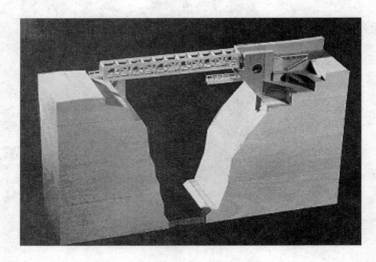

Fig. 6.4 Site Contour Ⅱ

Steep site contours may be modeled as a section of property limited to the area of focus.

New Words and Expressions

model	['mɔdəl]	n.	模型；设计；型号
interchangeable	[ˌintə'tʃeindʒəbl]	a.	可交换的，可互换的，可交替的
massing	['mæsiŋ]	n.	块化，密集，集中
presentation	[ˌprezən'teiʃən]	n.	显示，呈现，表现，描述
refinement	[ri'fainmənt]	n.	精炼的产品，精细的改进
resolved	[ri'zɔlvd]	a.	下定决心的，断然的
primary	['praiməri]	a.	首要的；主要的；基本的；最初的
secondary	['sekəndəri]	a.	次要的，次等的
void	[vɔid]	a.	空的，空虚的
component	[kəm'pəunənt]	n.	成分；组成部分；部件；元件

contour ['kɔntuə]	n.	外形，轮廓
entourage [ˌɔntu'raːʒ]	n.	周围，环境；随从
foliage ['fəuliidʒ]	n.	叶饰；植物的叶子(总称)；叶子
facade [fə'saːd]	n.	(房屋的)正面；假象；外观
medium ['miːdjəm]	n.	媒介；手段，方法，工具
phase [feiz]	n.	阶段，时期
spontaneity [ˌspɔntə'niːiti]	n.	自发性，自动
visualize ['viʒuəlaiz]	vt.	设想，想象
alignment [ə'lainmənt]	n.	定线，线向，路线
proportion [prə'pɔːʃən]	n.	均衡；协调；比例
spatial ['speiʃəl]	a.	空间的，立体空间的，三维空间的
chipboard ['tʃipbɔːd]	n.	硬纸板，纸板
proposition [ˌprɔpə'ziʃən]	n.	论点；主张；建议；提案
circulation [ˌsəːkju'leiʃən]	n.	通道；环流；流通
increment ['inkrimənt]	n.	增加，增量
serve as		被用作……，充当……，起……的作用
be open to		向……开放

Unit 7

Building Structures

Text: Structural Types of Building

The part of the building that holds up the weight and load is called the structural part. Parts, such as windows, that do not hold up the building are the non-structural parts. Buildings fall into two very broad structural types because of the different ways that buildings are made to hold up weight. These types are as follow.

(1) The frame structure(Fig. 7.1 and Fig. 7.2), where is frame or skeleton, holds up the weight and other materials are used to close the building up. Frame structures can be made of wood, materials such us concrete.

Fig. 7.1　Frame Structure Ⅰ

Fig. 7.2　Frame Structure Ⅱ

(2) Mass wall types (Fig. 7.3), where solid materials such as concrete, brick and other types of masonry are used to build heavy walls that hold up the building. This type can be made of brick, stone, and separate concrete and monolithic concrete parts.

Fig. 7.3　Mass Wall Building—Notre Dame Cathedral in Paris

Frame Structural Types

Frame structures are built more than mass wall building. Making a frame building in its broadest sense is simply making a frame that holds up the roof and the walls. The walls are added to the frame and do not act as load-bearing or supporting parts. The floors are suspended between the frame parts. In this manner the frame building has a foundation and the frame to hold up all the other parts of the building. Frame buildings range from small tool sheds to giant skyscrapers. Homes, schools, and factories may all be made with frames. The types of materials used to make the frames for buildings include wood, steel, aluminum and concrete. Other types of materials may also be used under special conditions. Building frames often have parts made of two or more types of materials such as wood and aluminum, mixed together.

Mass Wall Types

Many buildings are made without frames. The walls of these buildings are made of some strong substance such as concrete, brick or stone. The walls must be strong and solid to support the loads of the floors and the roof. Mass walls are very strong and durable. Walls made of brick or mud have lasted for hundreds and even thousands of years. Ancient mass wall buildings include the Pyramids of Egypt, the Coliseum of Rome, Notre Dame Cathedral in Paris, and the cliff dwellings of the ancient Indians of the southwestern United States.

However, walls made in this manner cost a lot in terms of both material and work. They take longer to build and not so comfortable to live in, unless special care is taken to insulate the insides of the walls. Mass walls were used to build the cold stone castles that knights lived in. These have been known for centuries as cold drafty places. The knights used to hang large rugs on the walls to make rooms warmer.

In modern times, however, changes have been made. Although walls are still sometimes made from solid stone, other ways are used more often. Concrete blocks are used to make walls because they are easy to handle and are lighter in weight than stone. The concrete blocks are then veneered with brick or stone for beauty.

Concrete is also widely used for modern mass walls. All of the openings for windows and doors are made when the wall is poured.

Today mass walls are not cold, just as castle walls were hundreds of years ago. Today, however, people need not hang rugs over the walls to be warm. Furring strips are put on inside the wall. Insulation is placed between the strips and covered with SAN inside wall of panels or drywall. The insulation makes a much better way of keeping a room warm than just hanging a rug over the stone.

New Words and Expressions

non-structural [ˈnɔnˈstrʌktʃərəl]	a.		非结构的
frame [freim]	n.		框架
skeleton [ˈskelitn]	n.		骨架；框架
solid [ˈsɔlid]	a.		结实的，稳定的，坚固的

Building Structures Unit 7

masonry	['meisənri]	n.	砖石建筑，砌石工程
monolithic	[ˌmɔnə'liθik]	n.	整体的
mass	[mæs]	n.	团，块，堆
load-bearing	['ləud'bɛəriŋ]	a.	承重的
suspend	[sə'spend]	vt.	悬，挂，吊
shed	[ʃed]	n.	棚，库
skyscraper	['skaiˌskreipə]	n.	摩天大楼
aluminum	[ˌælju:'minjəm]	n.	铝
substance	['sʌbstəns]	n.	物质
durable	['djuərəbl]	a.	持久的，耐用的
last	[lɑ:st]	vi.	持续，延续
mud	[mʌd]	n.	泥
coliseum	[ˌkɔli'siəm]	n.	大体育馆，大剧场，大公共娱乐场
cathedral	[kə'θi:drəl]	n.	大教堂
cliff	[klif]	n.	悬崖；峭壁
dwelling	['dweliŋ]	n.	住处，处所
inside	['in'said]	a.	内部的；里面的；内侧的
castle	['kɑ:sl]	n.	城堡，堡垒
knight	[nait]	n.	（中古时代的）武士，骑士
drafty	['drɑ:fti]	n.	通风良好的，有缝隙风吹入的
rug	[rʌg]	n.	地毯；壁毯
veneer	[vi'niə]	vt.	在（某物表面）上加薄片镶饰

opening ['əupəniŋ]	n.	洞；缺口
pour [pɔː]	n.	浇注，浇铸
furring ['fəːriŋ]	n.	板条，垫高料
strip [strip]	n.	条状，带状
panel ['pænəl]	n.	护墙板，镶板
drywall [drai'wɔːl]		干砌墙壁，清水墙
hold up		支撑
fall into		分成
frame structure		框架结构
mass wall		实体墙
close up		围护
in this manner		这样，这样一来；用这种方式
be mixed together		把……混合在一起
just as		正像，正如
furring strips		钉罩面板的木条
Coliseum of Rome		罗马斗兽场
Notre Dame Cathedral in Paris		巴黎圣母院
cliff dwellings		岩屋

Notes

1. Buildings fall into two very broad structural types because of the different ways that buildings are made to hold up weight.

   that 引导了一个定语从句，修饰 ways，其作用相当于 in which，在从句中做状语；to hold up weight 在定语从句中作目的状语。

2. Making a frame building in its broadest sense is simply making a frame that holds up the roof and the walls.

    第一个动名词短语 Making... 在句子中做主语；第二个动名词短语 making... 在句子中作表语。in its broadest sense：从最广泛意义上说。

3. In this manner the frame building has a foundation and the frame to hold up all the other parts of the building.

    to hold up all the other parts of the building 为动词不定式，作后置定语，修饰 a foundation and the frame。

4. ... just as castle walls were hundreds of years ago.

    were 后面省略了 cold 一词。

Exercises

Ⅰ. Answer the following questions according to the text.

1. What is the structural part of buildings?
2. How do buildings fall into two broad structural types?
3. What are the differences between frame structure and mass wall types?
4. What are functions of frame and wall in a frame building?
5. Which material can be used to make the frames for buildings?
6. Which buildings belong to mass wall buildings?
7. Are there disadvantages of mass wall types?
8. How have changes been made for mass wall types in modern times?

Ⅱ. Translate the following terms into Chinese.

1. structural types
2. frame structure
3. frame building
4. mass wall types
5. heavy wall
6. to insulate the insides of the walls
7. concrete blocks
8. furring strips

参考译文

建筑结构类型

建筑物中承受重量和荷载的部分称之为建筑结构部分,而不承载建筑物重量的部分如窗户等为非结构部分。由于建筑物支撑重量的方式不同,它们可分为两大结构类型。这些类型如下。

第一,框架结构,如图7.1和7.2所示。在这种结构中,框架或骨架支撑建筑物的重量,其他材料用于围护建筑物。框架结构由木料和其他材料如混凝土等构成。

图7.1　框架结构 Ⅰ

图7.2　框架结构 Ⅱ

第二,实体墙类型,如图7.3所示。混凝土、砖头和其他砌石等坚实的材料用于建造支撑建筑物的厚壁墙,这种类型的墙由砖头、石块、单一混凝土和整体浇灌混凝土建成。

图7.3　实体墙建筑——巴黎圣母院

框架结构类型

　　框架结构建筑物比实体墙建筑物的建造更多。从最广泛意义上说,框架建筑物的建造仅仅是建造一个支撑屋顶和墙体的框架。墙体附加在框架上,不起承重或支撑的作用,楼板悬垂于框架间。这样,框架建筑物就有了支撑其他所有部分的基础和框架。框架建筑物涵盖的范围极广,小到工具棚,大到摩天大楼。住房、学校和工厂可能都是框架结构。用于建造框架的建筑材料有木材、钢材、铝材和混凝土,在特殊条件下也可使用其他类型的材料。建筑物框架有些部分通常又由两种或多种材料如木材、铝材,木材、铝材混合型材料等建造而成。

实体墙类型

　　许多没有框架的建筑物,其墙壁由非常坚固的材料如混凝土、砖头或石料砌成。墙体必须坚固结实以支撑楼板和屋顶的荷重。实体墙非常坚固耐用,有些用砖或泥砌成的墙已有几百年,甚至几千年的历史。古代实体墙建筑有埃及金字塔、罗马斗兽场、巴黎圣母院和美国西南部印第安人岩屋。

　　尽管如此,就材料和工程而言,以这种方式砌成的墙花费颇多,不仅费时,而且居住并不舒适,除非特别注意墙内部的隔热。实体墙过去用来建造骑士居住的冰冷城堡,几世纪来这类建筑一直被称为冒冷风之地,过去,骑士们经常把壁毯挂在墙上以使房间暖和些。

　　不管怎样,现代已发生了很多变化。尽管有时墙壁还用坚固的石料砌成,但其他方法用得更多一些。混凝土砌块用来砌墙,因为它们易于处理,重量也比石料轻。混凝土砌块表面还可以镶嵌砖片或石片以示美观。

　　混凝土也被广泛用来砌现代的实体墙。浇筑墙体时,会留出所有门、窗的开口。

　　如今的实体墙不像几百年前的城堡墙那么冰冷。无论如何,今天的人们无需在墙壁上挂壁毯取暖了。墙壁内部可放置钉罩面板的木条,在木条间可放置隔热材料,并在护墙板或清水墙内的隔热材料上撒上一层苯乙烯。比起在石墙上挂壁毯,隔热是保持屋内暖和的更好方法。

Reading Material: Underground Construction

　　Underground construction has been around for thousands of years, mostly developed through mining and more recently through transport, housing and commercial industries. The Channel

Tunnel, London Underground, British Library and various shopping centers are all examples of underground construction.

Underground housing (sometimes called earth sheltered housing) refers specifically to homes that have been built underground, either partially or completely. These subterranean homes have grown increasingly popular over the last thirty years and are an important sector in the green building movement.

Thousands of people in Europe and America live in underground homes. In Russia there is more development below the ground than above it. Countries like Japan and China, where development space is at a premium, are particularly keen to build underground living places. In the UK, the movement is much slower, with less than a hundred underground homes in existence. This is partly due to a misinformed belief that underground homes are dirty, damp, dark, claustrophobic and unstable places to live in. But it is also due to a lack of guidance and information about building regulations and specifications, and a lack of knowledge about their potential as a sustainable building practice.

Underground Dwelling Design

To a certain extent the design of an underground home is determined by the conditions of the site. Soil type, topography, precipitation, ground water levels, load—bearing properties and slope stability all need to be carefully considered. Construction materials need to be waterproof, durable and strong enough to withstand underground pressure (concrete is frequently used). Water is a particular consideration in underground building, and special drainage techniques may need to be implemented around the site, particularly along the roof areas.

There are several methods of building for subterranean living:

Constructed Caves—made by tunneling into the earth. Although popular around the world, this can be an expensive and dangerous procedure.

Cut and Cover—also called culvert homes, these are made by assembling precast concrete pipes and containers into the required design of the living space, and then burying them in the ground.

Earth Berm—house is first built on flat land or a small hill, and then buried, leaving a wall or roof open for light.

Elevational—house is built into the side of a hill with the front of the home left open.

Atrium—also called courtyard homes, the rooms are built below the ground around a sunken garden or courtyard that lets light in.

PSP—stands for post, shoring and polyethylene. House is built by excavating the ground, sinking in posts, placing shoring(boards) between the posts and the earth, and placing polyethylene plastic sheets(for waterproofing) behind the shoring.

Shaft—an ambitious project in Japan called Alice City plans the construction of a wide and deep cylindrical shaft sunk into the earth with a domed skylight covering, and different levels for business and domestic use built around the shaft.

All underground homes need well-designed ventilation systems to control indoor air quality and humidity. Natural daylight design using light atriums, shafts and wells can also be used to improve the quality of underground living.

Advantages of Underground Buildings

Underground houses have many advantages over conventional housing. Unlike conventional homes, they can be built on steep surfaces and can maximize space in small areas by going below the ground. In addition, the materials excavated in construction can be used in the building process.

Underground houses have less surface area so fewer building materials are used, and maintenance costs are lower. They are also wind, fire and earthquake resistant, providing a secure and safe environment in extreme weather.

One of the greatest benefits of underground living is energy efficiency. The earth's subsurface temperature remains stable, so underground dwellings benefit from geothermal mass and heat exchange, staying cool in the summer and warm in the winter. This saves around 80% in energy costs. By incorporating solar design this energy bill can be reduced to zero, providing hot water and heat to the home all year round. An additional benefit of the surrounding earth is noise insulation. Underground homes are exceptionally quiet places to live in.

Finally, underground houses blend with the natural landscape, and have minimum impact on the local ecology. This is not only aesthetically pleasing but ensures that the maximum habitat is left alone for wildlife.

Designing Down for a Sustainable Future

Underground construction is not a new industry, but it is often overlooked as a design strategy for sustainable building. A well-designed underground home can be a stylish, comfortable, secure, bright and inspiring place to live in. More than that, it is an excellent example of the ecohome ideal, demonstrating energy efficiency, low-impact design and harmony with its natural surroundings. With the increasing demand for more development sites and ever-diminishing green spaces, along with the enforcement of stricter regulations for greener homes, building underground seems the obvious way down.

New Words and Expressions

underground ['ʌndəgraund]	a.	地下的；地下组织的；秘密的
	ad.	在地下；秘密地
mining ['mainiŋ]	n.	采矿（业）
subterranean [ˌsʌbtə'reiniən]	a.	地表下面的；地下的
sector ['sektə]	n.	部门；领域
premium ['pri:miəm]	n.	奖；奖金；额外费用；保险费
damp [dæmp]	a.	潮湿的，不完全干燥的
	n.	潮湿，湿气
claustrophobic [ˌklɔ:strə'fəubik]	a.	患幽闭恐惧症的；导致幽闭恐惧症的
specification [ˌspesifi'keiʃən]	n.	规格；规格说明；规范；详细说明
topography [tə'pɔgrəfi]	n.	地形，地貌，地势；地形学；地形测量学
precipitation [priˌsipi'teiʃən]	n.	（雨等）降落；某地区降雨等的量
waterproof ['wɔ:təpru:f]	a.	不透水的，防水的
	vt.	使防水；使不透水
implement ['implimənt]	vt.	使生效，贯彻，执行
culvert ['kʌlvət]	n.	管路
container [kən'teinə]	n.	容器；集装箱，货柜
berm [bə:m]	n.	台坎；（防御工事等的）护堤
atrium ['eitriəm]	n.	天井前厅；中庭
sunken ['sʌŋkən]	a.	低于周围平面的，凹陷的；下陷的

shoring ['ʃɔːriŋ]	n.	利用支柱的支撑，支柱
polyethylene [ˌpɔliˈeθiliːn]	n.	聚乙烯
shaft [ʃɑːft]	n.	井状通道；通风井；(电梯的)升降机井
cylindrical [siˈlindrikəl]	a.	圆柱形的；圆筒状的
domestic [dəˈmestik]	a.	家庭的，家用的；本国的，国内的
humidity [hjuːˈmiditi]	n.	湿度，潮湿，湿气
excavate [ˈekskəveit]	vt.	挖掘，开凿；挖出，发掘
maintenance [ˈmeintinəns]	n.	维持；维护；保养；维修
resistant [riˈzistənt]	a.	有抵抗力的，抵抗的
geothermal [ˌdʒiəuˈθəməl]	a.	地热的，地温的；地热(或地温)产生的
blend [blend]	vt. & vi.	(使)混合，(使)混杂
maximum [ˈmæksiməm]	n.	最大的量、体积、强度等
	a.	最大值的，最大量的
minimum [ˈminiməm]	a.	最低的，最小的
	n.	最低限度，最小量
habitat [ˈhæbitæt]	n.	(动物的)栖息地，住处
stylish [ˈstailiʃ]	a.	有风度的，有气派的，有格调的
secure [siˈkjuə]	a.	安全的，无危险的，牢固的；稳当的；牢靠的
enforcement [inˈfɔːsmənt]	n.	强制，实施，执行
at a premium		非常珍贵；非常需要；渴求
along with		和，同，与……一道；加之；除某物以外
in existence		存在

Unit 8

Building Facilities

Text: Classification of Construction Equipment

The various types of construction equipment can be grouped in several ways for the sake of discussion. One way of classifying equipment is to group it by the function it performs in the construction process. In this way, such dissimilar equipment as scrapers, front-end loaders and belt conveyors can be classified as equipment that loads, carries and dumps loose material. Another way of classifying equipment is by the construction operations in which it is used; for example, scrapers, dozers, belt loaders and off-the-road haulers are generally used in earthmoving operations.

Functional Classification of Equipment

A functional classification of construction equipment includes power units; tractors; loaders, haulers, and other kinds of material-handing equipment; many kinds of material-processing equipment.

Power units. The common sources of power for construction equipment are internal combustion engines, electric generators, hydraulic pumps, air compressors and steam boilers shown from Fig. 8.1 to Fig. 8.5. Internal combustion engines are used to drive most large, mobile earthmoving machines, cranes, haulers, front-end loaders, graders and so on. They are also the source of power for electric generators, air compressors and hydraulic pumps. Electric motors are used to operate some of the large, less mobile shovels and to drive belt conveyors. Compressed air is used to operate hand tools and pumps, and air compressors and steam boilers provide power to pile hammers. Hydraulic power is used to drive the front-end operating machinery on cranes and excavators and the operating parts of scrapers such as the apron and the material ejector.

Fig. 8.1   Internal Combustion Engine

Fig. 8.2   Electric Generator

Fig. 8.3   Hydraulic Pump

Fig. 8.4   Air Compressor

Fig. 8.5   Steam Boiler

Prime movers. Prime movers are another functional group of equipment and they make it possible for the machinery to operate. Prime movers translate the output of power units into work. The term prime mover has been used to describe the power unit, the power train between the power unit and the driving wheels or gears, and the type of mounting of the equipment. One form of prime mover is the crawler-track or rubber-tired mounting that moves self-propelled equipment. For stationary equipment the prime moving parts may be cables, chains, or belts driven by a power unit. Or the prime mover may be the energy of compressed air or hydraulic fluids moving in pipes or hoses. A more complete prime mover is needed to move equipment that is not self-propelled. For instance, a crawler or rubber-tired tractor shown in Fig. 8.6 is a prime mover that may be used to tow a scraper, a wagon, a compactor, or a trailer for moving other equipment.

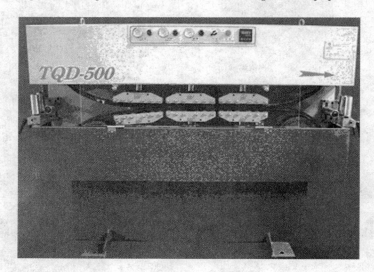

Fig. 8.6 Crawler Tractor

Fig. 8.7 Bulldozer

Excavating equipment. Another group of equipment is used to excavate rock and earth. This group includes the several forms of tractor-mounted bulldozers shown in Fig. 8.7—the straight blade, the universal blade, the angle blade and so on. A similar machine is the motor grader that shapes and grades the ground surface. Either of these machines can be equipped to rip or scarify material to be excavated. Front-end loaders, power shovels, backhoes, draglines and clamshells are used to excavate and load rock and soil. Elevating graders, belt excavators, trenchers, dredgers and tunnelers are more specialized machines that also perform this function. Another type of equipment is used to install structural elements into or to remove material from the ground. Pile drivers, extractors, caisson hole drills, well drills and wagon drills are in this group.

Material-handling equipment. There are several groups of material-handling equipment that differ in what the equipment does with the material it handles. Included in the categories of material handling equipment are the various cranes—mobile cranes, tower cranes (Fig. 8.8) and so on-that lift materials vertically or pick them up and move them at short distances horizontally. More specialized machines of this sort are the lumber and pipe carriers. Another group of construction equipment is used to move loose or processed material such as earth, sand and wet concrete. In general, this sort of equipment must be loaded by other equipment, but it can dump the loose material. This group includes belt, bucket, screw conveyors and haulers-dump-trucks and rear-dump wagons.

Fig. 8.8 Tower Crane

Fig. 8.9 Feeder

Material processing equipment. Material processing equipment is used to produce graded aggregates from natural rock and gravel for base course material, graded fill, portland cement, bituminous concrete and asphalt. The aggregates and the cementitious and other ingredients are mixed in other material-processing equipment to make soil-cement, concrete or bituminous paving materials. To process aggregates there are feeders (Fig. 8.9), grizzlies, screens and various kinds of crushers-jaw, gyratory, roll, impact and hammer mill. For the mixing processes there are storage bins, cement silos, batchers, concrete mixers, pavers and asphalt mixing plants.

Placing and finishing equipment. To place processed material in their final locations, another group of construction equipment is required. These machines place the material uniformly and compactly to achieved the specified results. The equipment used to place and finish processed materials includes concrete spreaders(Fig. 8. 10), screeds, asphalt pavers, graders and compactors.

Fig. 8. 10　Concrete Spreader

New Words and Expressions

scraper	['skreipə]	n.	刮刀；平土机；铲土机
conveyor	[kən'veiə]	n.	传送带；传送装置
dump	[dʌmp]	vt.	倾倒，倾卸
dozer	['dəuzə]	n.	推土机
hauler	['hɔːlə]	n.	起吊机
functional	['fʌŋkʃənəl]	a.	能起作用的，正常运转的
combustion	[kəm'bʌstʃən]	n.	燃烧，烧毁；燃烧过程
crane	[krein]	n.	起重机，吊车
excavator	['ekskə,veitə]	n.	挖掘机
apron	['eiprən]	n.	停机坪
ejector	[i'dʒektə]	n.	喷射器，排出器
prime	[praim]	a.	首要的；主要的；基本的
mount	[maunt]	n.	安装，装配
crawler-track	['krɔːlə'træk]	n.	履带传动
stationary	['steiʃənəri]	a.	不动的，固定的
tow	[təu]	vt.	拖，拉，拽

bulldozer ['bul,dəuzə]	n.	推土机
rip [rip]	vt.	锯开，割裂
scarify ['skɛərifai]	vt.	切割；软化
backhoe ['bækhəu]	n.	反铲挖土机
dragline ['dræglain]	n.	标记，符号；标志；迹象
clamshell ['klæmʃel]	n.	蛤壳式挖泥机
trencher ['trentʃə]	n.	挖沟机
dredger ['dredʒə]	n.	挖泥机，挖泥船
tunneler ['tʌnələ]	n.	隧道掘进机
caisson ['keisən]	n.	(水下作业用的)沉箱
lumber ['lʌmbə]	n.	木材；成材
aggregate ['ægrigeit]	vt.	聚集，集合
asphalt ['æs,fɔ:lt]	n.	沥青；柏油
gravel ['grævəl]	n.	砂砾，砾石
bituminous [bi'tju:minəs]	a.	含沥青的
bin [bin]	n.	仓，料架
silo ['sailəu]	n.	筒仓
batcher ['bætʃə]	n.	混凝土材料计量器
uniformly ['ju:nifɔ:mli]	ad.	一致地；均匀地
screed [skri:d]	n.	(定墙上灰泥厚薄的)准条；匀泥尺，样板
be grouped in		被分为
for the sake of		为了；为了……的利益
differ in		在……方面不同

Notes

1. Another way of classifying equipment is by the construction operations in which it is used; for example, scrapers, dozers, belt loaders, and off – the – road haulers are generally used in earthmoving operations.

   另一种方式是按照使用设备所进行的建筑工程来分类的,例如,铲土机、推土机、带式传送机以及卷扬机通常用在大量掘土的工程中。

   the construction operations in which it is used 是指在其过程中使用设备的建筑工程。

2. Prime movers are another functional group of equipment; they make it possible for the machinery to operate.

   原动力装置是又一类按功能划分的设备,这类设备用来转动机器。

   make it possible 直译为"使某件事成为可能"。

3. Either of these machines can be equipped to rip or scarify material to be excavated.

   这类机器都可以装配设备来对被挖掘的物料进行割裂或划切。

   either of 指机器中的任意一类。

4. There are several groups of material – handling equipment that differ in what the equipment does with the material it handles.

   有几类物料搬运设备,这些设备根据它们对物料所作的处理而有所不同。

   differ in 意思是在某方面有所不同,也就是指在设备对物料的处理方面。

Exercises

Ⅰ. Answer the following questions according to the text.

1. How are the various types of construction equipment be grouped?
2. What does a functional classification of construction equipment include?
3. What are internal combustion engines used for?
4. According to the text, what does the term prime mover refer to?
5. What are the different sources of power such as internal combustion engines, electric generators, hydraulic pumps, air compressors and steam boilers used for?
6. For stationary equipment what the prime moving parts may be?
7. What is a motor grader used for and which type of construction equipment it is?
8. Can you give examples of some more specialized machines that perform the function of excavating?

9. What do material-handling equipment differ in?

10. What kind of material processing equipment can be used for the mixing process?

Ⅱ. Translate the following terms into Chinese.

1. functional classification

2. hydraulic power

3. prime mover

4. storage bin

5. screw conveyor

6. dump – truck

7. rear – dump wagon

8. graded fill

9. asphalt mixing plant

10. asphalt paver

参考译文

建筑设备的分类

为了便于讨论，可以用几种方式对各种建筑设备加以分类。其中一种方式是按照设备在建筑过程中发挥的功能来进行分类的。按这种方式，像铲土机、前端式装载机以及带式传送机这些不同的设备，便可归为装载、运送和倾卸松散物料的设备类别中。另一种方式是按照使用设备所进行的建筑工程来分类的，例如，铲土机、推土机、带式传送机以及卷扬机通常用在大量掘土的工程中。

按功能分类设备

按功能分类的建筑设备包括动力设备，牵引车，装载机、卷扬机及其他物料装卸设备，各种物料加工设备。

动力设备。建筑设备的动力源一般有内燃机、发电机、液压泵、空气压缩机及蒸汽锅炉，如图8.1～图8.5所示。大多数大型可移动泥土挖掘机械、起重机、起吊机、前端式装载机、平土机等设备一般用内燃机作动力。发电机、空气压缩机和液压泵也用内燃机作为动力源。电动机一般用以驱动一些大型的、不常移动的铲车和带式传送机。手用工具和泵一般用压缩空气作动力，而打桩机则用空气压缩机和蒸汽锅炉来提供动力。挖掘机和起重机上的前端式操作装置以及像停机坪和物料抛掷器等刮土机的操作部件一般使用液压动力。

图8.1 内燃机

图8.2 发电机

图8.3 液压泵

图8.4 空气压缩机

图8.5 蒸汽锅炉

原动力装置。原动力装置是又一类按功能划分的设备，这类设备用来转动机器。原动力装置将动力装置输出的能量转化为做功。原动力装置一词被用来指动力装置、动力装置与传动轮或齿轮之间的传动系统以及设备的装配类型。履带式或橡胶轮胎式装配便是一种原动力装配方式，这种装置用来推进机动式设备。对于固定不动的设备，其原动力装置可能是钢索、链条，或由动力装置驱动的传送带。或者，由压缩空气或液压体在管筒中运动而产生的能量也可以作为原动力。对于一台非机动式设备，则需要有更完善的原动力装置来运转。例如，图8.6所示的履带式牵引机，或橡胶轮胎式牵引机便是一种用来牵引刮土机、四轮货车、夯土机或拖车，以移动其他设备的原动力装置。

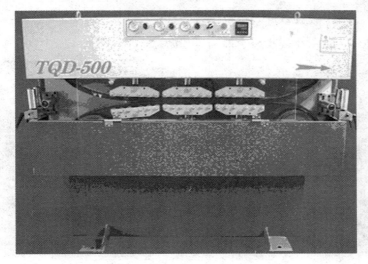

图8.6 履带式牵引机

挖掘设备。另一类是用来挖掘石子和泥土的设备。如图8.7所示，这类设备包括几种牵引式推土机——直铲、通用铲、角铲等。电动平土机是一种类似的机器，它用来定型和平整地面。这类机器都可以装配设备来对被挖掘的物料进行割裂或划切。前端式装载机、电铲、反向铲、拉铲挖土机及蛤壳式挖泥机用来挖掘和装载石子与泥土。一些更为专业化的机器，如升降式平土机、履带式挖掘机、挖沟机、挖泥机和隧道掘进机，也具有这一功能。还有一类设备，用来将构件安装到地面或将物料从地面移走。打桩机、挖掘机、沉箱钻机、钻井机和车装饰机均属于此类设备。

图8.7 推土机

物料搬运设备。有几类物料搬运设备，这些设备根据他们对物料所作的处理而有所不同。此类设备包括各种吊车——移动吊车、塔吊等，如图8.8所示，用来上下垂直运送物料或抓吊物料进行短距离水平移动。此类设备中还有更为专业的机器，如木材搬运车和管道搬运车。另一种类型的建筑设备用来运送松散的或经过加工的物料，如泥土、沙石和塑性混凝土。通常，这类设备须由其他设备荷载，但他们对松散物料可以卸。此类设备包括履带式、翻斗式、螺旋式输送机和拖运车——自卸卡车和后卸车。

物料加工设备。物料加工设备用来将天然的石子和砂砾加工成分级骨料，以在地基用料、分级填充、硅酸盐水泥、沥青混凝土和柏油中使用。骨料和胶结性及其他材料要在另外的物料加工设备中进行混合，制成水泥加固土、混凝土或沥青铺砌材料。如图8.9所示，加工骨料的机器有喂料机、格筛、滤网，以及各种碎石机——颚式碎石机、回转式碎石机、滚动式碎石机、碰撞式碎石机及锤式碎石机。在做混合处理时，还有漏斗箱、水泥筒仓、配料计量器、混凝土搅拌机、摊铺机和沥青搅拌装置。

图8.8 塔吊

图8.9 喂料机

铺放设备和精整设备。要把加工好的物料铺放到最终位置，还需要另一类建筑设备。这些机器均匀、细密地对物料进行安放，以达到指定结果。用来铺放和精整加工好的物料的设备包括混凝土摊铺机（如图8.10所示）、样板、沥青摊铺机、平整机和夯实机。

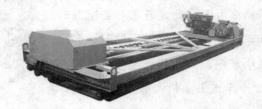

图8.10 混凝土摊铺机

Reading Material：Choosing Construction Equipment

Equipment is a vital factor in construction, particularly in the heavy and highway segments of the construction industry where it may be the largest long-term capital investment of many companies. Heavy, highway and utilities jobs may have relatively large quantities of excavation, grading, embankment construction, aggregate production and mass concrete construction, which all require large, heavy and very expensive pieces of equipment. Financial planning in construction companies focuses on decisions relating purchasing, leasing, depreciating, maintaining, repairing and replacing equipment. The choice of construction equipment determines the method of doing the work, the time to compete the work and the cost of construction.

The main objective of successful construction project management is to satisfy the requirements of the plans and specifications, within the time allowed by the contract documents, for the least possible cost. One of the keys to success is the control of the time, cost and quality by the selection and use of the right equipment for the job. In order to select equipment to perform the work for the least cost, the character and quantity of work to be performed and the production rates and costs of various kinds of equipment must be known. The character and quantity of the work are established by the contract documents and the condition and location of the job site. The capabilities of construction machines are described in the equipment specifications; and the costs that must be considered are the costs of owning, leasing, or renting the equipment and the costs of operating, maintaining and repairing it.

All construction equipment designed to handle or process material in one form or another. The material may be rock, which must be loosened, loaded, hauled, dumped, crushed, screened and washed to produce aggregate for paving materials or concrete. It may be undisturbed earth, which must be loosened, loaded, hauled, dumped, spread, shaped and compacted to construct an embankment. It may be cement, aggregate, water and admixtures that must be stored, batched, mixed, transported, placed, finished and cured to build a concrete structure. It may be water that must be removed from a construction site to permit work to be done in the dry. Or it may be structural steel that must be hoisted to erect a building. Different machines are required to perform each of these tasks, and the appropriate machine is determined by the job to be done.

Equipment manufacturers publish specifications that indicate the capabilities of their machines. Specifications provide the information needed to determine if equipment can do the work. This information includes such things as the payloads of hauling units, the weights of pile hammers, the sizes of bulldozer blades, the digging depths of excavators, the tipping loads of front-end loaders and the weights of compactors. Specifications also contain information needed to determine the production rates of the machines, including the travel speeds of trucks and tractors in various gears, the volumes of the drums of concrete mixers and the capacities of pumps and belt conveyors.

New Words and Expressions

segment ['segmənt]	n.	部分，片段
vital ['vaitəl]	a.	极重要的，必不可少的
relatively ['rel'ətivli]	ad.	相对地；相比较而言
embankment [em'bæŋkmənt]	n.	路堤；河堤
depreciate [di'pri:ʃi:,eit]	vt.	贬值，跌价
objective [əb'dʒektiv]	n.	目标，目的
capability [,keipə'biliti]	n.	容量；性能
admixture [æd'mikstʃə]	n.	混合物；附加剂
hoist [hɔist]	vt. & n.	吊起；举起；起重机械
appropriate [ə'prəupriət]	a.	合适的，恰当的
indicate ['indikeit]	vt.	标出，显示
payload ['pei,ləud]	n.	载荷，装载量
undisturbed earth		坚硬泥土
tipping load		倾覆载荷

Unit 9

Building Construction Management

Text: Construction Management

Construction management (CM) offers a way for architecture firms to expand their services, increase income, and control the construction process while maintaining a professional relationship with their clients. More control of the project schedule, improved integration of design and construction, and daily on-site construction coordination can result in cost savings for the owner and increased profitability for the architect (Fig. 9.1). *The business of architecture—2006 AIA Firm Survey* indicates that billings for CM services are 23.6 percent of total billings, second only to those for design-bid-build, the most common method of project delivery.

Fig. 9.1 What Construction Management Involves

There are two primary models for providing CM services—CM-adviser and CM-constructor. The CM-adviser model can sometimes be limited to consultation for constructability and cost management. CM-agent is a variation of the CM-adviser model in which the construction manager is authorized to enter into contracts on behalf of the owner. CM-constructor model is similar to design-build project delivery.

Elements of Construction Management

CM services embody a cluster of activities related to construction scheduling, construction cost estimating, and contractor coordination, among others (Fig. 9.2). Construction managers must be totally familiar with the services included in the owner-construction manager agreement for each project. They must also clearly understand the general conditions of the contract that outline the roles played by the owner, the architect, the contractor and the construction manager.

Fig. 9.2 Construction Planning and Coordination

Scheduling. Two types of schedules are referenced in owner-architect construction management contracts: the project schedule and the construction schedule.

The project schedule is prepared as early as possible in preconstruction phases of project development. The architect is in the best position to lead in the preparation of this document. Input from all the parties—including the owner, architect, and construction manager—is needed to establish meaningful dates for completing the design, contract documents and construction work. The construction phase shown in the project schedule can be general in nature, primarily noting construction start and completion dates.

The construction manager prepares the construction schedule during the construction documents phase. This schedule should be included in the specifications so bidders can use it when preparing their bids. The construction manager maintains and updates the schedule as it evolves during the construction phase.

Scheduling is one of the most important procedures for a successful CM process. Schedules organize the forces and direct the energies of all project participants toward the successful completion of a project.

Preconstruction activities. Preconstruction activities comprise all work done by the architect during the schematic and design development phases. The construction manager works closely with the design architect during this phase to aid in the completion of the project design. The construction manager's tasks include estimating costs, advising on materials and equipment, writing specifications, scheduling construction work and reviewing bidders' qualifications.

As noted in *AIA BB01/CMa—1992 (B131—2008), Standard Form of Agreement Between Owner and Construction Manager*, the construction manager prepares preliminary construction cost estimates based on schematic designs. As the project design progresses, the construction manager updates the estimates and advises the owner and architect if it appears the construction cost may exceed the approved project budget.

Bidding/negotiation activities. A primary difference between a CM-adviser method and a conventional design-bid-build project delivery is the breakdown of the work into a number of bid packages rather than a single prime contract. Depending on the complexity and nature of the work, the actual number of bid packages can vary from as few as four to as many as thirty or more. The CM-constructor method, on the other hand, performs like a negotiated conventional single-prime project, either cost-plus or with a guaranteed maximum price (GMP). In either case, for the best results, open biding should be pursued, with the owner and architect participating in the selection of the subcontractors.

Construction phase activities. The construction manager's responsibility is to coordinate the efforts of the contractors, while the project architect continues to make all design-related decisions. The construction manager and project architect continue to work closely during construction. General progress, change orders and contractor applications for payment need review and approval by both the construction manager and architect. Although the construction phase activity centers on the construction manager, the project architect still provides contract administration services as specified in the owner-architect agreement. In projects without a construction manager, architects sometimes provide coordination activities above and beyond basic contract administration services in order to successfully complete the project delivery.

New Words and Expressions

expand [ik'spænd]	vt. & vi.	扩大，增大，增加，增强，扩展
coordinate [kəu'ɔːdineit]	v.	协调；协同动作
profitability [ˌprɔfitə'biləti]	n.	盈利性
billing ['biliŋ]	n.	业务量
authorize ['ɔːθəraiz]	vt.	授权；委任；委托；批准；认可
element ['elimənt]	n.	元素；要素，成分
embody [im'bɔdi]	vt.	体现；包括，包含
cluster ['klʌstə]	n.	群，堆，组，团，串
owner ['əunə]	n.	物主；业主
evolve [i'vɔlv]	vi. & vt.	演变；进化；发展
participant [pɑː'tisipənt]	n.	参加者，参与者
completion [kəm'pliːʃən]	n.	完成；竣工
comprise [kəm'praiz]	vt.	包括，包含；构成；组成
schematic [skiː'mætik]	a.	图表的；图解的
bidder ['bidə]	n.	投标者，投标商
complexity [kəm'pleksiti]	n.	复杂性
qualification [ˌkwɔlifi'keiʃən]	n.	资格；资历
exceed [ik'siːd]	vt.	超过
guarantee [ˌgærən'tiː]	vt.	担保；保证
subcontractor [ˌsʌbkən'træktə]	n.	分包商
cost saving		成本节约
on behalf of		代表
cost plus		成本加成
change order		工程变更通知单

Notes

1. Construction management (CM) offers a way for architecture firms to expand their services, increase income, and control the construction process while maintaining a professional relationship with their clients.

   施工管理为建筑公司提供了在扩展其服务、增加收入以及控制施工过程的同时，与客户保持一种专业性人际关系的方式。

   句中 expand their services, increase income, and control the construction process 为 way 的后置定语。

2. CM services embody a cluster of activities related to construction scheduling, construction cost estimating, and contractor coordination, among others.

   施工管理服务包括很多活动，除了其他的，主要有和施工进度、施工成本估算和承包方的协调等相关的活动。

3. Schedules organize the forces and direct the energies of all project participants toward the successful completion of a project.

   施工进度计划能组织各方面的力量并引导各个项目参与者成功完成项目。

4. Depending on the complexity and nature of the work, the actual number of bid packages canvary from as few as four to as many as thirty or more.

   根据工程的复杂程度和特点，标段的实际数量少到 4 个、多到 30 个或更多。

5. Although the construction phase activity centers on the construction manager, the project architect still provides contract administration services as specified in the owner-architect agreement.

   虽然施工阶段的活动主要集中在施工经理一方，项目建筑师仍然要按照业主—建筑师协议的规定提供合同管理服务。

   在句中，as 引导一个限制性定语从句，先行词为 contract administration services。

Exercises

Ⅰ. Answer the following questions according to the text.

1. According to paragraph 1, what is the importance of construction management?
2. How many models are there for providing CM services? What are they?
3. What activities are embodied in CM services? What is construction manager required to do?
4. Who is in the best position to lead in the preparation of project schedules?
5. When should the construction schedule be prepared?

6. What is the importance of scheduling?

7. What are construction manager's tasks in preconstruction activities?

8. What is the primary difference between a CM-adviser method and a conventional design-bid-build project delivery?

9. During the construction phase, what is the construction manager's responsibility?

10. In projects without a construction manager, what are architects supposed to do?

Ⅱ. Translate the following terms into Chinese.

1. construction management

2. construction documents phase

3. design development phase

4. construction manager

5. construction cost

6. project budget

参考译文

施工管理

图9.1 施工管理的内容

施工管理(CM)为建筑公司提供了在扩展其服务、增加收入以及控制施工过程的同时,与客户保持一种专业性人际关系的方式。对项目进度更多的控制,设计与施工更进一步的融合以及日常现场施工协调,可以为业主节省成本并为建筑师获得更多的盈利(图9.1)。《建筑业——2006年美国建筑师协会公司调查》表明,施工管理的业务量占业务总量的23.6%,仅次于最常用的项目交付方式,即设计—招标—建筑模式的业务总量。

提供施工管理服务有两种基本模式——工程咨询项目管理和工程施工项目管理。工程咨询项目管理有时会局限在可建设性和成本管理的咨询方面。施工管理代理是工程咨询项目管理模式的另一种形式,在这种模式中,施工经理被授权代表业主参与到合同中。工程施工项目管理和设计—建造的项目交付方式相似。

施工管理的要素

施工管理服务包括很多活动，除了其他的，主要有和施工进度、施工成本估算和承包方的协调等相关的活动(图9.2)。施工经理必须完全熟悉包含在每一个工程中的业主—施工经理协议中的服务项目。他们也必须对业主、建筑师、承包方和施工经理的角色做出概述的合同的基本条款有清楚的理解。

进度安排。在业主—建筑师施工管理合同中有两种进度安排方式，即项目进度安排和施工进度安排。

项目进度安排要尽可能早地在项目施工前期准备好。建筑师带头准备项目进度安排的最佳人选。各方的投入——包括业主、建筑师和施工经理都需要为完成设计、合同文件和施工等工作确定一个合理的日期。在项目进度中的建设实施阶段实际上可以比较概括，主要是注明施工开始和结束的日期。

施工经理要在施工图设计阶段准备好施工进度安排。这个进度安排应该包含在细则里面，这样投标人可以在准备投标的时候使用。在工程施工阶段，施工经理随着施工的进展维护和更新进度表。

图9.2 施工规划与协作

进度安排是成功的施工管理过程中的一个重要步骤。施工进度计划能组织各方面的力量并引导各个项目参与者成功完成项目。

施工前的活动。施工前期活动包括建筑师在策划和技术设计阶段所做的所有工作。在这一阶段，施工经理和设计师紧密配合来辅助完成项目的设计。施工经理的任务包括成本的估算、材料和设备的建议，细则的编写，施工进度的安排和投标者的资格审查。

按照在《美国建筑师协会 B 系列 B01/工程咨询项目管理—1992(B131—2008)，业主与施工经理协议的标准形式》中提到的，施工经理按照方案设计准备初步的施工成本估算。随着项目设计的进展，项目施工经理更新这些估算数据，如果施工成本超出了批准的项目预算，施工经理应该给业主和建筑师提供建议。

招标/谈判活动。工程咨询项目管理模式和传统的设计—招标—建筑的项目交付模式之间最基本的区别就在于它把项目分成若干个标段，而不是单个的主合同。根据工程的复杂程度和特点，标段的实际数量少到 4 个、多到 30 个或更多。在另一方面，工程施工项目管理的方法就像是谈判后的传统的单个主项目，可以是成本加成也可以是最高价格保证的形式。不论在哪种情况下，为了取得最好的结果，应进行公开招标，业主和建筑师都应该参加分包商的挑选。

施工阶段的活动。施工经理的责任是要协调各承包方的力量，而项目建筑师继续作出与设计的决定。在施工过程中，施工经理和项目建筑师要继续紧密合作。总体进度、工程变更通知单、承包商的支付申请，需要施工经理和建筑师共同审查和批准。虽然施工阶段的活动主要集中在施工经理一方，项目建筑师仍然要按照业主—建筑师协议的规定提供合同管理服务。在没有施工经理的项目中，为了成功完成项目交付，有时建筑师要进行超过基本合同管理服务的协调工作。

Reading Material: The Architect as Construction Manager

Why should architect provide CM services? In traditional project delivery, architects are subject to many forces beyond their control that can greatly affect both design decisions and the financial outcome of the project. In the design-bid-build approach, the contractor drives the construction schedule and the architect's time during the construction period. The longer a project runs, the more time the architect must spend, resulting in reduced profit. Contractor-led design-build may place the architect under the contractor's control, which can affect both the design quality and the architect's income. When a third-party construction manager, separated from the architect for the project, serves as the owner's agent, design challenges and time-consuming reevaluations can sometimes result, placing the architect in a defensive position rather than a position as the owner's trusted agent.

As an integral part of architecture practice, CM services can often yield the following positive outcomes.

● *Reduced project costs*. Subcontractor prices can be passed directly to the owner without prime contractor markup or general superintendent costs.

● *Substantially reduced construction time*. Proper scheduling and management allow faster construction while high-quality design and construction are maintained.

- *Daily job site representation by the architect.* The architect visits the job site with no additional cost to the project.
- *A single source of responsibility.* When the architect of record also provides CM services, the client has one point of contact for both design and construction.
- *Avoidance of adversarial relationships.* Provision of both design and CM services by the architect promotes collaborative relationships between the architect and prime contractors and independent construction managers.
- *Increased earnings for the architect.* The architect's earnings are greater without the need to increase the number of projects in the office.

Risks and Rewards

Like most professional services, construction management has risks associated with it. An understanding of those risks is important when design firms decide to make construction management part of their services. With this understanding there is a better chance to fully capture the rewards of construction management as reflected in more efficient project delivery, improved client relationships and greater financial returns.

Risks of CM services. Architect-led CM adviser services are professional services just as the architect's traditional design work is, thus they carry similar professional liability risks. Standard professional liability insurance can provide coverage for architects offering CM-adviser services just as it does for design services. However, some additional exposure to job site safety issues could exist ever though contractors hold this responsibility as they do in the design-bid-build method.

Job site safety is the greatest concern for the architect engaging in CM-adviser services. The courts might assign responsibility for job site safety to the construction manager, even though the primary duty of the construction manager is coordinating the efforts of the contractors, rather than the means and methods of construction. The general conditions of the contract for CM work very clearly note that responsibility for safety rests with the contractors. Even so, the construction manager may have liability exposure here. Such exposure can be reduced by initiating a proactive job site safety program and by securing contractor-type liability insurance for CM work. With CM-constructor work, job site risk and construction means and methods must be assumed; however, this increased income. Again, a proactive job site safety program and the addition of contractor's liability insurance can help the architect address these increased risks.

Rewards of architect-led CM. CM services can yield a high net profit (often about 50 percent of the gross fee) plus increasing the return for design service. Projects can be completed as much as 25 percent sooner using a CM approach, allowing designers to move on to new projects sooner and thus increase production for the firm.

One firm found when it added architect-led CM-adviser services to its service offerings, the net income derived from traditional design-bid-build services increased from 10 percent to as much as 30 percent or more. When the firm used the architect-led CM-constructor method, its net income increased as much as 50 percent. These financial rewards are in addition to the benefit of eliminating adversarial relationships with general contractors and independent CM-advisers and CM-constructors working directly for the owner.

New Words and Expressions

financial [fai'nænʃəl]	a.	财政的，财务的，金融的
profit ['prɔfit]	n.	收益；利润；赢利
defensive [di'fensiv]	a.	防御用的；防御性的
integral ['intigrəl]	a.	构成整体所必需的；完整的
superintendent [ˌsjuːpərin'tendənt]	n.	管理员，指挥人，总段长
avoidance [ə'vɔidəns]	n.	避免
adversarial [ˌædvə'sɛəriəl]	a.	敌手的；对手的；对抗的
collaborative [kə'læbərətiv]	a.	协作的，合作的
capture ['kæptʃə]	vt.	俘获；夺取；赢得；捕捉
liability [ˌlaiə'biliti]	n.	责任
insurance [in'ʃuərəns]	n.	保险，保险费
coverage ['kʌvəridʒ]	n.	覆盖范围；覆盖程度
exposure [iks'pəuʒə]	n.	暴露；揭露；揭发；曝光
engage [in'geidʒ]	v.	参加；从事
initiate [i'niʃieit]	vt.	发起，创始，开始

proactive [prəuˈæktiv]	a.	有前瞻性的；先发制人的；先行一步的；积极的
fee [fi:]	n.	费，酬金
eliminate [iˈlimineit]	vt.	消除，清除，排除
third-party		第三方；第三当事人
prime contractor		总承包人
job site		工地，施工现场
rest with		是……的责任
net profit		纯利润

Unit 10

Energy-saving Buildings

Text: Low Carbon Buildings—Target Zero Carbon Construction

Most of our energy comes from burning fossil fuels. This produces Carbon Dioxide and pollution, and uses up a valuable and diminishing resource. Whatever the truth about the proportion of global warming caused by man compared to natural causes, there is no doubt that we are burning more hydrocarbon fuels and causing more pollution than ever before. This impacts climate change and causes environmental degradation.

Buildings account for about half of the total fuel burn in the country and half of that is accounted for by commercial buildings. As more fossil fuels are extracted, the demand for them grows, which results in the price increasing. Most fossil fuels are now imported, leading to dependency. So there are very sensible economic and political cases for reducing hydrocarbon, or fossil fuel consumption. Unless buildings become more efficient, there is no way the political target of an 80% carbon reduction by 2050 will be met.

How to Embody Less Carbon Construction Materials in Your Building

Concrete and steel both emit carbon dioxide in their production. If all steel used in the building project were new and made from imported ore in a blast furnace, then the carbon content within the steel would be as high as in concrete. Fortunately steel is nearly 100% recyclable, and the re-use embodies much less carbon. Therefore, steel framed buildings and structures embody less carbon than their concrete cousins.

Using timber framing is an alternative and unlike steel and concrete, the production of timber absorbs carbon dioxide from the atmosphere. Apart from the energy spent in harvesting, transporting and processing the timber is therefore carbon-negative. If all the timber at the end of its life were to be burnt in a waste-to-power plant, the use of timber would be very positive. But timber has an Achilles'heel. Only a small proportion of a tree becomes structural timber. Wood that rots gives off part of its carbon content as methane, which is 25 times more dangerous as a greenhouse gas, than carbon dioxide. If only 4% of a tree rots in this way, its global warming potential is the same as the burning of a whole tree. Timber frame is also very expensive, and is best kept for those places where the aesthetic value is great. Thus steel buildings in practice usually embody low carbon.

How to Make Commercial Buildings More Efficient in Use

A. Reducing the amount of air leakage.

B. Doors can have rapid opening and closing to minimize the time they are open.

C. Reducing thermal bridging.

D. Efficient lighting and internal equipment will reduce energy use.

E. Various wall finishes on south facing walls can trap heat which can be used for space heating.

F. Buildings can be built with "green roofs" (Fig. 10.1) with insulation and then a membrane, over which soil or other growing medium is placed. Then suitable plants are planted.

Fig. 10.1　Building with "Green Roofs"

How to Get Power From Sources Other Than Hydrocarbons

A. Ground Source Heat Pumps—Use pipes buried in the ground to circulate water over large areas. This can extract heat from the ground (Fig. 10.2).

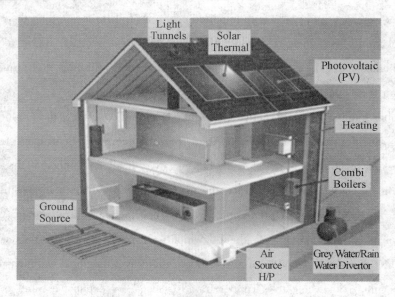

Fig. 10.2 Low Carbon Building Designed in this Fashion

B. Air Source Heat Pumps—By extracting heat from the outside to heat buildings.

C. Combined Heat and Power, CHP—Generating both electricity and useful heat with the appliance of a heat engine or power station.

D. Biomass Fuelled Power Stations—This renewable energy source is derived from various energy sources such as wood, waste, landfill gases, alcohol fuels and rubbish.

E. Solar Heating—These systems are a popular way of using renewable energy technology. This can work effectively for heating water, but probably not for space heating or cooling.

F. Solar Power Generation—This source of electricity is produced from the sun and pushes it into existing electrical grids.

G. Photo voltaic Cells—This is a direct conversion from light to electricity.

H. Hydro Electric—A good clean method of generating electricity assuming there is a good head of water. It can be done on a small scale if there is a supply of high pressured water.

I. Wave Power—This is an almost inexhaustible source of energy but it is still in its infancy.

J. Tidal Power—Uses the power of the tides to convert energy into electricity or other forms of power.

K. Purchasing "Green" Energy—By producing your own energy and using natural resources, this electricity or heat can be described as zero or low carbon energy.

New Words and Expressions

carbon ['kɑːbən]	n.	碳
fossil ['fɔsl]	n.	化石
fuel [fjuəl]	n.	燃料
diminish [di'miniʃ]	vi.	变小；变少；缩小；减少；降低
hydrocarbon [,haidrəu'kɑːbən]	n.	烃；碳氢化合物
impact ['impækt]	vt.	影响
degradation [,degrə'deiʃən]	n.	降低；恶化；堕落
consumption [kən'sʌmpʃən]	n.	消耗量，消费量；消耗，消费
steel [stiːl]	n.	钢
emit [i'mit]	vt.	发射，放射，发出；排出；排泄
dioxide [dai'ɔksaid]	n.	二氧化物
ore [ɔː]	n.	矿，矿石
timber ['timbə]	n.	木材，木料
Achilles' heel [ə'kiliːz,hiː]		弱点
rot [rɔt]	vi.	腐烂；腐坏
methane ['meθein]	n.	沼气，甲烷
aesthetic [iːs'θetik]	a.	美学的；悦目的；艺术的；雅致的
insulation [,insju'leiʃən]	n.	隔离，隔绝；绝缘；隔热
membrane ['membrein]	n.	薄膜，振动片，表层
circulate ['səːkjuleit]	vi.	循环
extract [ik'strækt]	vt.	抽出；提炼；提取

appliance [ə'plaiəns]	n.	工具；用具；器具；器械
biomass ['baiəumæs]	n.	生物量；生物质
conversion [kən'və:ʃən]	n.	转变；变换
inexhaustible [,inig'zɔ:stəbl]	a.	无穷尽的；用不完的
infancy ['infənsi]	n.	婴儿期；幼儿期；初期
blast furnace		高炉，鼓风炉

Notes

1. Whatever the truth about the proportion of global warming caused by man compared to natural causes, there is no doubt that we are burning more hydrocarbon fuels and causing more pollution than ever before.

   不管人为引起的全球变暖与自然因素导致的全球变暖相比，它的比重有多少，毫无疑问，人们在史无前例地燃烧更多的烃类燃料并引起更多的污染。

2. As more fossil fuels are extracted, the demand for them grows, which results in the price increasing.

   当人们提炼更多的矿物燃料时，对它的需求就会增长，这就导致了价格的上涨。

   result in：导致，结果是。

   e.g. The talks resulted in reducing the number of missiles. 谈判结果削减了导弹数量。

3. If all steel used in the building project were new and made from imported ore in a blast furnace, then the carbon content within the steel would be as high as in concrete.

   如果在建筑项目中使用的所有钢材都是新的，并且是在锻炉中从进口矿石中提炼出来的，那么钢材中碳的含量将和混凝土中的含量一样高。

4. Apart from the energy spent in harvesting, transporting and processing, the timber is therefore carbon-negative.

   因此，除了收获、运输和加工的能量消耗，木材是碳负性的。

   apart from：除了……都；除去。

   e.g. Apart from his nose, he's quite good-looking. 他除了鼻子以外，哪儿都很好看。

5. But timber has an Achilles'heel.

   但是木材也有它的致命的弱点，句中 Achilles'heel 指某人或某物致命的弱点或缺陷。这个词来源于希腊神话中的英雄人物阿基琉斯。阿基琉斯在年幼时，他母亲将他浸在了斯提克斯河（冥河）中，这就能让他不会受伤。他母亲当时是抓着他的脚后跟把他放入水中的，而他的脚后跟没有浸到水里面。后来，阿基琉斯脚后跟被箭射中而死去。

Exercises

Ⅰ. Answer the following questions according to the text.

1. Where does most of our energy come from?
2. What are the disadvantages of burning fossil fuels?
3. Why is it important to embody less carbon construction materials in the building?
4. If all steel used in the building project were new and made from imported ore in a blast furnace, what will be the result?
5. Why do steel framed buildings and structures embody less carbon than the concrete ones?
6. What is the advantage of using timber framing?
7. What is the disadvantage of timber?
8. How can we make commercial buildings more efficient in use?

Ⅱ. Translate the following terms into Chinese.

1. fossil fuel
2. hydrocarbon fuel
3. commercial building
4. steel framed building
5. ground source heat pump
6. air source heat pump
7. wave power
8. tidal power

参考译文

低碳建筑——以零排放建筑为目标

人们应用的多数的能量来自于燃烧矿物燃料，这就会产生二氧化碳和污染并会用尽宝贵而且日渐减少的资源。不管人为引起的全球变暖与自然因素导致的全球变暖相比，它的比重有多少，毫无疑问，人们在史无前例地燃烧更多的烃类燃料并引起更多的污染。这会影响气候变化并导致环境恶化。

建筑物消耗的燃料占全国燃料消耗总量的一半，这一半中又有一半被商业建筑所消耗。当人们提炼更多的矿物燃料时，对它的需求就会增长，这就导致了价格的上涨。大多数的矿物燃料现在都是靠进口，这又导致了依赖性，所以有许多很理性的经济和政治事件是减少烃类或矿物燃料的消耗的。除非建筑物更为高效，到2050年80%的碳减排的政治目标就无法完成。

在建筑物中如何包含更少的碳建筑材料

混凝土和钢材在生产过程中都会排放出二氧化碳。如果在建筑项目中使用的所有钢材都是新的，并且是在锻炉中从进口矿石中提炼出来的，那么钢材中碳的含量将和混凝土中的含量一样高。幸运的是钢材几乎是可以百分之百循环利用的，这种再利用的钢材包含了较少的碳。因此，钢结构的建筑和结构比混凝土结构包含的碳少。

使用木结构是另一种选择，不像钢筋和混凝土，木材的生产会从大气中吸收二氧化碳。因此，除了收获、运输和加工的能量消耗，木材是碳负性的。如果所有的木材在寿命期结束后都能用于废物焚烧发电厂，则木材的使用将有着非常积极的作用。但是木材也有它的致命的弱点，一棵树只有很少的一部分能用做结构木材。腐烂的木头会将一部分碳以甲烷的形式释放出来，作为温室气体，这要比二氧化碳危险25倍。如果一棵树的4%以这种方式腐烂，其使全球变暖的潜在性就相当于燃烧一整棵树。木结构也非常的昂贵，最好用在那些具有非常重要的美学价值的建筑。因此，钢结构建筑实际应用中含低碳。

如何让商业建筑在使用中更为高效

图10.1　带有"绿色屋顶"的建筑

A. 减少漏风量。
B. 让门迅速地开关以将它们打开的时间减少到最短。
C. 减少热桥。
D. 高效的采光和室内设备会减少能量使用。
E. 南面墙的各种整饰可以吸收热量，这可以用于房间供暖。
F. 建筑物可以用隔热材料建筑"绿色房顶"（图10.1），然后铺上薄膜，再在上面放置土壤或其他生长基质，最后种植合适的植物。

如何从能源而不是从烃类取得能量

A. 地源热泵——使用埋在地下的管道来使水在地下大面积循环,这可以从土壤中提取热量(图 10.2)。

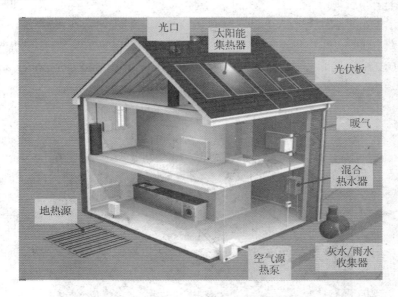

图 10.2 以低碳理念的设计的建筑

B. 空气源热泵——通过从户外吸收热量来加热建筑物。

C. 热电联产——用热机装置或发电厂在发电的同时产生有用的热量。

D. 生物质燃料发电厂——这种可再生能源来自各种能源,如木头、废物、填埋区沼气、酒精燃料和垃圾等。

E. 太阳能供暖——这些系统是使用可再生能源技术常用的方式,可以很有效地用来烧水,但或许不太适用于室内供暖或降温。

F. 太阳能发电——这种电能产生自太阳并被输送进现有的电网。

G. 光伏电池——这是一种直接由光能向电能转化的方法。

H. 水力发电——如果有大量水源,那么这是一种清洁的发电方式。如果有高压水,那么也可以小规模发电。

I. 波浪发电——这几乎是一种用之不竭的能源,但仍在探索期。

J. 潮汐发电——将潮汐的能量转化成电力或其他形式的能量。

K. 购买"绿色能源"——制造自己的能源或使用天然资源,这种电能或热能被称为零碳或低碳能源。

Reading Material: Green Buildings

What is Green

The term "green" refers to environmentally practices from building design to the landscaping choices(Fig. 10. 3). It also encompasses energy use, water use, and stormwater and wastewater reuse.

Fig. 10. 3 A Green Building

Building can be rated for their environmentally sustainable construction. One such rating system is the LEED(Leadership in Energy and Environmental Design). This building rating system is developed by the U. S. Green Building Council(GBC)and is created to:

- Define "green buildings" by establishing a common standard of measurement.
- Promote integrated, whole-building design practice.
- Recognize environmental leadership in the building industry.
- Stimulate green competition.
- Raise consumer awareness of green buildings benefits.
- Transform the standard building market to a green building market.

GBC members, representing every sector of the building industry, develop and continue to refine LEED. The rating system addresses six major areas:

1. Sustainable sites
2. Water efficiency
3. Energy and atmosphere

4. Materials and resources

5. Indoor environmental quality

6. Innovation and design process

The terms "green" and "green buildings" apply not just to products, but to construction strategies, building design and orientation, land building operations, maintenance and more. The less impact a building has on human health and the environment, the more green it is.

Why Going Green Makes Sense

A green building may cost more up front but, in the long run, will save money through lower operating costs over the life of the building. The green building approach applies a project lifecycle cost analysis to determining the appropriate up-front expenditure. This analytical method calculates costs over the useful life of the asset.

The integrated systems approach ensures that the building is designed as one system rather than stand-alone systems. Some benefits, such as improving occupant health, comfort, productivity, reducing pollution and landfill waste, are not easily quantified. Consequently, they are not adequately considered in cost analysis. For this reason, consider setting aside a small portion of the building budgets to cover differential cost associated with less tangible green building benefits or to cover the cost of researching and analyzing green building options. Even with a tight budget, many green measures can be incorporated with minimal up-front costs, and they can yield enormous savings.

Retrofitting Existing Buildings

It's not impossible to transform an existing building to a green one, but it can be difficult. There are some easy items that can be retrofitted into an existing building at relatively low cost and, in time, often pay for the retrofit. Existing buildings require an up-front investment to replace something that already exists and is, presumably, in working order. However, not all of the necessary alterations need to be done at once.

Start with what needs to be fixed or repaired such as leaking faucets or toilets(Fig. 10.4). If the building is being remodeled, keep the green concept in mind and use recycled material and paints that are environment friendly. Whether the building is old or new, installing low-flow fixtures is one of the easiest ways to save money and to conserve water.

If leaking faucet or fixtures cannot be repaired, replace them with ultra-low-flow fixtures.

Fig. 10. 4　Repair the Leaking Faucets to Make Your Home Green

Some of the easiest green retrofits to an existing building are methods for decreasing power usage and water consumption. For example, anytime a light bulb burns out, replace it with an ultra-low-energy use bulb (Fig. 10. 5). When landscaping, use native plants and garden designs that requires less (or no) irrigation.

Fig. 10. 5　Energy-saving Lamp

New Buildings

Location is as important in green building as it is in real estate. Drinking water treatment plants are usually located near the water source—and with luck, out of the 100-year flood plain. The billing office, however, may be located in a more central place for customer convenience, which can mean using less gas to get there.

Try to orient the building for the best environmental fit, such as positioning the building to take advantage of the sun or leaving as much of the natural landscape, including tress and other plant life as possible. Set the elevation of the building to minimize earthwork and balance the earth to be removed with the earth to be filled. If there are any wetlands, do not disturb them. It takes many years for nature to make topsoil. Save it; Don't waste it.

Take into account all of the utilities that you may need to extend to the building, keeping distance to a minimum. Consider where entrance or exit roads are placed. And keep the road grade to a minimum. Take advantage of the prevailing wind direction for wind turbines.

  The building itself can have many green options—from using recycled building material, to paints and finishes that have fewer (or no) chemicals, to heating and cooling the building, to using as much natural sunlight as possible.

New Words and Expressions

encompass	[in'kʌmpəs]	vt.	包含；包括；包围
stormwater	[stɔːm'wɔːtə]	n.	暴雨水
rate	[reit]	vt.	评定；评价
stimulate	['stimjuleit]	vt.	刺激；激励；激发
innovation	[ˌinə'veiʃən]	n.	革新，创新
appropriate	[ə'prəupriət]	a.	适当的；合适的；正当的
expenditure	[ik'spenditʃə]	n.	经费，开支，费用
asset	['æset]	n.	有价值的人或物；优点；财产
landfill	['lændfil]	n.	垃圾填埋；垃圾填埋地
quantify	['kwɔntiˌfai]	vt.	确定……的数量，量化
differential	[ˌdifə'renʃəl]	a.	不同的；有分别的；基于差别的
tangible	['tændʒəbəl]	a.	明确的；确切的；真实的；可触知的
incorporate	[in'kɔːpəreit]	vt.	包括；包含；合并
retrofit	['retrəfit]	vt.	更新；改进；改型；改造
presumably	[pri'zjuːməbli]	ad.	大概，可能，据推测
alteration	[ˌɔːltə'reiʃən]	n.	改变，变更，修改
fixture	['fikstʃə]	n.	固定装置
faucet	['fɔːsit]	n.	<美>水龙头
position	[pə'ziʃən]	vt.	安置；定位

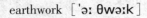

earthwork ['ə:θwə:k]	n.	土方量，土方工程
wetland ['wetlænd]	n.	湿地；沼地
topsoil ['tɔp,sɔil]	n.	表层土
utility [ju:'tiliti]	n.	有用；实用；效用；[pl.] 公用设施
turbine ['tə:bin]	n.	涡轮机；透平机
take sth. into account		计及；斟酌；体谅；考虑
take advantage of		利用，运用
natural landscape		自然景观
prevailing wind direction		盛行风向

Vocabulary

New Words and Expressions

abode [ə'bəud]	n.	住所，公寓
above all		首先，尤其是，最重要的是
accuracy ['ækjurəsi]	n.	正确性，准确，精度，准确度；精密性
Achilles'heel [ə'kili:z‚hi:l]		弱点
adjoin [ə'dʒɔin]	vt. & vi.	邻近，毗连
adjoining [ə‚dʒɔiniŋ]	a.	毗邻的，邻接的；伴随的
administration [əd‚minis'treiʃən]	n.	管理，经营，支配；实行，执行
administrator [əd'ministreitə]	n.	管理人；行政人员
admixture [æd‚mikstʃə]	n.	混合物；附加剂
adob [ə'dəubi]	n.	砖坯，土砖
adversarial [‚ædvə'sɛəriəl]	a.	敌手的；对手的；对抗的
advisable [əd'vaizəbl]	a.	可取；明智
aerial ['ɛəriəl]	a.	空气的，空中的

aerial photography			空中摄影，空中照相术
aesthetic [iːsˈθetik]		a.	有关美的，美学的；悦目的；审美的；雅致的
aesthetically [iːsˈθetikəli]		ad.	审美地，美学观点上地
affect [əˈfekt]		vt.	影响
agent [ˈeidʒənt]		n.	作用剂；作用者，原动力，动因
aggregate [ˈæɡriɡeit]		n.	（拌水泥用的）粒料，骨料
		vt.	聚集，集合
agreement [əˈɡriːmənt]		n.	契约，合同，协议，一致；符合
alignment [əˈlainmənt]		n.	定线，线向，路线
along with			和，同，与……一道；加之；除某物以外
alter [ˈɔːltə]		vt.	改变；更改，变更；修改
alteration [ˌɔːltəˈreiʃən]		n.	改变，变更，修改
aluminum [əːljuːminəm]		n.	铝
amend [əˈmend]		vt.	改正；改善；改进
analyze [ˈænəlaiz]		vt.	分析，分解，解释
ancestral [ænˈsestrəl]		a.	祖先的，祖宗传下来的
anti-termite [ˌæntiˈtəːmait]		n.	防白蚁
anticipate [ænˈtisipeit]		vt.	预期，期望；预料；预先考虑到
antiquity [ænˈtikwiti]		n.	古老，年代久远，古物，古代
appliance [əˈplaiəns]		n.	工具；用具；器具；器械
appraisal [əˈpreizəl]		n.	估计，估量；评价；鉴定
appropriate [əˈprəupriət]		a.	合适的，恰当的
apron [ˈeiprən]		n.	停机坪
aqueduct [ˈækwiˌdʌkt]		n.	高架渠；导水管；渡槽

New Words and Expressions — Vocabulary

arch [ɑːtʃ]	n.	拱，拱门
architectural [ˌɑːkiˈtektʃərəl]	a.	建筑上的；建筑学的
arrange [əˈreindʒ]	n.	安排；准备，筹划；整理；布置
as of now		到目前为止
as well as		也，又
ascertain [ˌæsəˈtein]	vt.	查明；弄清；确定
asphalt [ˈæsˌfɔːlt]	n.	沥青；柏油
asset [ˈæset]	n.	有价值的人或物；优点；财产
assurance [əˈʃuərəns]	n.	保证，担保；确信；把握，信心
asymmetrical [ˌeisiˈmetrikl]	a.	不均匀的，不对称的
at a premium		非常珍贵；非常需要；渴求
at fault		有责任；有错
atrium [ˈeitriəm]	n.	天井前厅；中庭
attach [əˈtætʃ]	vt.	附着，附属
authority [ɔːˈθɔriti]	n.	权力；权威；当局，官方；管理机构
authorize [ˈɔːθəraiz]	vt.	授权；委任；委托；批准；认可
automate [ˈɔːtəmeit]	vt. &vi.	（使）自动化
avant-garde [ˌævˈgɑːd]	n.	革新者，艺术上的先锋派
avoidance [əˈvɔidəns]	n.	避免
axes [ˈæksiːz]	n.	轴
bachelor of science		理学学士
backhoe [ˈbækhəu]	n.	反铲挖土机
backside building		后罩房
batcher [ˈbætʃə]	n.	混凝土材料计量器

be aware		意识到，注意
be based on		以……为基础，根据
be entrusted with		受委托做某事
be familiar with		对……熟悉
be grouped in		被分为
be mixed together		把……混合在一起
be open to		向……开放
be up to		由某人决定；是某人的责任
bench terrace		水平梯田
berm [bə:m]	n.	台坎；(防御工事等的)护堤
bidder ['bidə]	n.	投标者，投标商
billing ['biliŋ]	n.	业务量
bin [bin]	n.	仓，料架
binder ['baində]	n.	黏合剂，黏结剂
biomass ['baiəumæs]	n.	生物量；生物质
bituminous [bi'tju:minəs]	a.	含沥青的
blast furnace		高炉，鼓风炉
blend [blend]	vt. & vi	(使)混合，(使)混杂
bloom [blu:m]	n.	繁荣，兴盛，成长，大量出现
blueprint ['blu:'print]	n.	蓝图，设计图
bond [bɔnd]	n.	黏结；黏合；契约
brickwork ['brikwə:k]	n.	砌砖
budget ['bʌdʒit]	n.	预算
budgeting ['bʌdʒitiŋ]	n.	预定；预算

New Words and Expressions — Vocabulary

bulge [bʌldʒ]	vi.	鼓起；凸出	
bulldozer [bulˌdəuzə']	n.	推土机	
bungalow [ˈbʌŋgləu]	n.	平房；单层小屋	
buttress [ˈbʌtris]	n.	扶壁，扶垛	
by means of		用某办法；借助于某事物	
by way of		经过，经由；通过……的方法	
cable [ˈkeibl]	n.	缆，索，钢索	
cable-stayed bridge		斜拉桥	
caisson [ˈkeisən]	n.	（水下作业用的）沉箱	
canal [kəˈnæl]	n.	运河；沟渠	
canopy [ˈkænəpiː]	n.	华盖，罩篷	
capability [ˌkeipəˈbiliti]	n.	容量；性能	
capture [ˈkæptʃə]	vt.	俘获；夺取；赢得；捕捉	
carbon [ˈkɑːbən]	n.	碳	
carry out		实行，执行；完成，实现	
cartographer [kɑːˈtɔgrəfə]	n.	制图员	
cast [kɑːst]	vt.	投，扔，抛；浇铸	
castle [ˈkɑːsl]	n.	城堡，堡垒	
cathedral [kəˈθiːdrəl]	n.	大教堂	
cement [siˈment]	n.	水泥	
certificate [səˈtifikit]	n.	凭证，证书，证明书，执照	
change order		工程变更通知单	
characterize [ˈkæriktəraiz]	vt.	是……的特征，以……为特征	
chipboard [ˈtʃipbɔːd]	n.	硬纸板，纸板	

circulate	['səːkjuleit]	vi.	循环
circulation	[ˌsəːkju'leiʃən]	n.	通道；环流；流通
civil engineering			土木工程
clamshell	['klæmʃel]	n.	蛤壳式挖泥机
clause	[klɔːz]	n.	条款
claustrophobic	[ˌklɔːstrə'fəubik]	a.	患幽闭恐惧症的；导致幽闭恐惧症的
clay	[klei]	n.	黏土，泥土
client	['klaiənt]	n.	建设单位；委托人；买主，顾客
cliff	[klif]	n.	悬崖；峭壁
cliff dwellings			岩屋
close up			围护
cluster	['klʌstə]	n.	群，堆，组，团，串
code	[kəud]	n.	法律，规章，章程
coliseum	[ˌkɔli'siəm]	a.	大体育馆，大剧场，大公共娱乐场
Coliseum of Rome			罗马斗兽场
collaboration	[kəˌlæbə'reiʃən]	n.	合作，协作
collaborative	[kə'læbərətiv]	a.	协作的，合作的
collapse	[kə'læps]	vi.	倒坍，塌下；崩溃；突然失败
collective	[kə'lektiv]	a.	集体的，共同的，共有的
column	['kɔləm]	n.	柱，圆柱
combustion	[kəm'bʌstʃən]	n.	燃烧，烧毁；燃烧过程
commence	[kə'mens]	vt.	开始
commission	[kə'miʃən]	n.	任务；委托
compact	[kəm'pækt]	vt.	压紧，(使)坚实，把……紧压在一起

New Words and Expressions — Vocabulary

completion	[kəmˈpliːʃən]	n.	完成；竣工
complexity	[kəmˈpleksiti]	n.	复杂性
comply with			按要求、命令去做，依从，顺从，服从
component	[kəmˈpəunənt]	n.	成分；组成部分；部件；元件
composition	[ˌkɔmpəˈziʃən]	n.	构图；构成，成分
compression	[kəmˈpreʃən]	a.	挤压，压缩
compressive	[kəmˈpresiv]	a.	有压缩力的
comprise	[kəmˈpraiz]	vt.	包括，包含；构成；组成
concubine	[ˈkɔŋkjubain]	n.	妾，妃子
consensus	[kənˈsensəs]	n.	（意见等）一致，一致同意
consolidation	[kənˌsɔliˈdeiʃən]	n.	巩固，加强，强化
construct	[kənˈstrʌkt]	vt.	建筑；建造；构成；形成
construction engineering			建筑工程
construction material			建筑材料
consumption	[kənˈsʌmpʃən]	n.	消耗量，消费量；消耗，消费
container	[kənˈteinə]	n.	容器；集装箱，货柜
contemplate	[ˈkɔntempleit]	vt.	盘算，计议；周密考虑
contemporary	[kənˈtempərəri]	a.	当代的，同时代的，同属一个时期的
contour	[ˈkɔntuə]	n.	外形，轮廓
contractor	[kənˈtræktə]	n.	承包人，承包商
conversant	[ˈkɔnvəsənt]	a.	熟悉的，精通的
conversion	[kənˈvəːʃən]	n.	转变；变换
convey	[kənˈvei]	vt.	表达，转达；运输；运送
conveyor	[kənˈveiə]	n.	传送带；传送装置

coordinate [kəuˈɔːdiˈneit]	v.	协调；协同动作
copper door knockers		铜门环
cornice [ˈkɔːnis]	n.	檐口
cost plus		成本加成
cost saving		成本节约
coverage [ˈkʌvəridʒ]	n.	覆盖范围；覆盖程度
crane [krein]	n.	起重机，吊车
crawler-track [ˈkrɔːləˈtræk]	n.	履带传动
criminal negligence		过失犯罪
crisis [ˈkraisis]	n.	危机
culvert [ˈkʌlvət]	n.	管路
cumbersome [ˈkʌmbəsəm]	a.	笨重的；迟缓而缺乏效率的
curriculum [kəˈrikjuləm]	n.	课程
curve [kəːv]	n.	曲线，弧线
cylindrical [siˈlindrikəl]	a.	圆柱形的；圆筒状的
dam [dæm]	n.	水坝，堤，水闸
damp [dæmp]	a. n.	潮湿的，不完全干燥的 潮湿，湿气
deal with		论述，涉及
dedication [dediˈkeiʃən]	n.	忠诚；奉献
defect [diˈfekt]	n.	缺点；不足之处；毛病；瑕疵
defensive [diˈfensiv]	a.	防御用的；防御性的
degradation [ˌdegrəˈdeiʃən]	n.	降低；恶化；堕落
denote [diˈnəut]	vt.	指示，指出

New Words and Expressions — Vocabulary

depend on			依赖，依靠；取决于，随……而定
deplete	[diˈpliːt]	vt.	耗尽，使枯竭
depreciate	[diˈpriːʃiˌeit]	vt.	贬值，跌价
diachronic	[daiəˈkrɔnik]	a.	历时的
differ in			在……方面不同
differential	[ˌdifəˈrenʃəl]	a.	不同的；有分别的；基于差别的
differentiate	[ˌdifəˈrenʃieit]	vt. & vi.	区分，区别，辨别
differentiate from			指出……与……有区别
dimension	[diˈmenʃən]	n.	方面，特点；尺寸，大小；体积；范围
diminish	[diˈminiʃ]	v.	变小；变少；缩小；减少；降低
dioxide	[daiˈɔksaid]	n.	二氧化物
discipline	[ˈdisiplin]	n.	学科；教学科目
dispute	[disˈpjuːt]	n. & v.	争论，争端
distant	[ˈdistənt]	a.	（空间或时间）遥远的，远隔的
distinction	[disˈtiŋkʃən]	n.	区别，明显差别，特征
distinctive	[disˈtiŋktiv]	a.	有特色的，与众不同的
divergent	[daiˈvəːdʒənt]	a.	有分歧的；叉开的
diverse	[daiˈvəːs]	a.	不同的；多种多样的
divination	[ˌdiviˈneiʃən]	n.	预言
domain	[dəuˈmein]	n.	范围，领域
dome	[dəum]	n.	拱顶
domestic	[dəˈmestik]	a.	家庭的，家用的；本国的，国内的
dozer	[ˈdəuzə]	n.	推土机
draft	[drɑːft]	vt.	草拟，起草（文件）

drafty ['drɑːfti]	n.	通风良好的，有缝隙风吹入的
dragline ['dræglain]	n.	标记，符号；标志；迹象
drainage ['dreinidʒ]	n.	排水；排水设备
dredger ['dredʒə]	n.	挖泥机，挖泥船
drywall [drai'wɔːl]		干砌墙壁，清水墙
due to		因……而产生，（作为结果）发生
dump [dʌmp]	vt.	倾倒，倾卸
durability [ˌdjuərə'biləti]	n.	耐久性，耐用性
durable [ˌdjuərəbl]	a.	持久的，耐用的
dwelling ['dweliŋ]	n.	住处，处所
earthwork ['əːθwəːk]	n.	土方量，土方工程
eaves ['iːvz]	n.	屋檐
ecological [ˌekə'lɔdʒikəl]	a.	生态的；生态学的
edible ['edibl]	a.	可食的，食用的
ejector [i'dʒektə]	n.	喷射器，排出器
element ['elimənt]	n.	元素；要素，成分
eliminate [i'limineit]	vt.	消除，清除，排除
elitism [ei'liːtizm]	n.	精英主义；精英意识
embankment [em'bæŋkmənt]	n.	路堤；河堤
embody [im'bɔdi]	vt.	体现；包括，包含
emission [i'miʃən]	n.	排放（物）
emit [i'mit]	vt.	发射，放射，发出；排出；排泄
encompass [in'kʌmpəs]	vt.	包含；包括；包围
encounter [in'kauntə]	vt.	遇到，遭遇；偶然碰到，邂逅

enforcement [in'fɔːsmənt]		n.	强制，实施，执行
engage [in'geidʒ]		v.	参加；从事
engage in			参加，从事，忙于
engineering [ˌendʒi'niəriŋ]		n.	工程(学)，工程师行业
entire [in'taiə]		a.	全部的；整个的；完全的
entirely [in'taiəli]		ad.	完全地；彻底地
entourage [ˌɔntu'raːʒ]		n.	周围，环境；随从
envisage [in'vizidʒ]		vt.	想象，设想
essential [i'senʃəl]		a.	必要的；不可缺少的
evenly ['iːvənli]		ad.	均匀地；平坦地；平和地
evolve [i'vɔlv]		vi. & vt.	演变；进化；发展
excavate ['ekskəveit]		vt.	挖掘，开凿；挖出，发掘
excavator ['ekskəˌveitə]		n.	挖掘机
exceed [ik'siːd]		vt.	超过
expand [ik'spænd]		vt. & vi	扩大，增大，增加，增强，扩展
expenditure [ik'spenditʃə]		n.	经费，开支，费用
exposure [ik'spənʒə]		n.	暴露；揭露；揭发；曝光
extension [ik'stenʃən]		n.	伸长；延长；延展，伸展；增加；扩大
extract [ik'strækt]		vt.	抽出；提炼；提取
extrude [eks'truːd]		v.	挤压出，挤压成；突出，伸出；逐出
facade [fə'saːd]		n.	(房屋的)正面；假象；外观
facet ['fæsit]		n.	(问题等的)一个方面；(多面体的)面
facility [fə'siliti]		n.	设备，装备，工具
fall into			分成

famed [feimd]	a.	著名的	
faucet ['fɔ:sit]	n.	<美>水龙头	
fee [fi:]	n.	费，酬金	
financial [fai'nænʃəl]	a.	财政的，财务的，金融的	
fixture ['fikstʃə]	n.	固定装置	
foliage ['fəuliidʒ]	n.	叶饰；植物的叶子（总称）；叶子	
folklore ['fəuklɔ:]	n.	民间传统；民间故事；民俗	
for the sake of		为了；为了……的利益	
fossil ['fɔsl]	n.	化石	
foundation [faun'deiʃən]	n.	地基，房基	
frame [freim]	n.	框架	
frame structure		框架结构	
framework ['freimwə:k]	n.	骨架；构架工程；结构；框架	
fuel [fjuəl]	n.	燃料	
functional ['fʌŋkʃənəl]	a.	能起作用的，正常运转的	
furring ['fə:riŋ]	n.	板条，垫高料	
furring strips		钉罩面板的木条	
generate ['dʒenəreit]	vt.	生成，产生；引起，导致	
geometric [dʒiə'metrik]	a.	几何学的，图形的	
geometrically [dʒiə'metrikəli]	ad.	按几何学原理地；按几何图形地	
geometry [dʒi'ɔmitri]	n.	几何（学）	
geotechnical [,dʒiəu'teknikəl]	a.	土工的	
geothermal [,dʒiəu'θəməl]	a.	地热的，地温的；地热（或地温）产生的	

New Words and Expressions — Vocabulary

Gothic ['gɔθik]	a.	哥特式的
	n.	哥特式
graph [græf]	n.	图，图表，曲线图
graphical ['græfikəl]	a.	图解的；绘图的；生动的
gravel ['grævəl]	n.	砂砾，砾石
grid [grid]	n.	栅格，网格；地图的坐标方格；输电网
grillwork ['grilwə:k]	n.	格型图案
guarantee [ˌgærən'ti:]	vt.	担保；保证
habitable ['hæbitəbəl]	a.	适于居住的
habitat ['hæbitæt]	n.	（动物的）栖息地，住处
hauler ['hɔ:lə]	n.	起吊机
hazardous ['hæzədəs]	a.	冒险的，有危险的
herringbone ['heriŋbəun]	n.	鲱鱼鱼骨，交叉缝式，人字形
hoist [hɔist]	vt. & n.	吊起；举起；起重机械
hold up		支撑
hollow ['hɔləu]	a.	凹陷的；空的；中空的
horizontal [hɔri'zɔntl]	a.	平的；水平的；地平的
humidity [hju:'miditi]	n.	湿度，潮湿，湿气
hydraulic [hai'drɔ:lik]	a.	液力的，液压的
hydraulically [hai'drɔ:likəli]	ad.	通过水（或液）压
hydrocarbon [ˌhaidrəu'ka:bən]	n.	烃；碳氢化合物
identify [ai'dentifai]	vt.	识别，等同，标志
illustrate ['iləstreit]	vt.	说明，图解，举例说明
immense [i'mens]	a.	巨大的；广大的

impact ['impækt]	vt.	影响
impediment [im'pedimənt]	n.	妨碍、阻碍某事物进展或活动的人或物；身体上的某类残疾，缺陷
implement ['implimənt]	vt.	使生效，贯彻，执行
implicit [im'plisit]	a.	不言明的，含蓄的
in accordance with		与……一致，依照
in addition		另外，此外
in addition to		加之，除……之外
in advance of		提前；提早；预先；事先；在……之前
in depth		深入地，全面地
in existence		存在
in the case of		至于……，就……来说；就……而论
in this manner		这样，这样一来；用这种方式
in use		在使用中
incorporate [in'kɔːpəreit]	vt.	包括；包含；合并
increment ['inkrimənt]	n.	增加，增量
incur [in'kəː]	vt.	遭受；蒙受；招致；引起；带来
index ['indeks]	n.	指数，指标；索引，卡片索引，文献索引
indicate ['indikeit]	vt.	标出，显示
inexhaustible [ˌinig'zɔːstəbl]	a.	无穷尽的；用不完的
infancy ['infənsi]	n.	婴儿期；幼儿期；初期
infinite ['infinit]	a.	无限的，无穷的
infrastructure ['infrəˌstrʌktʃə]	n.	结构；基础设施
initially [i'niʃəli]	ad.	最初，开始

New Words and Expressions — Vocabulary

initiate	[i'niʃieit]	vt.	发起，创始，开始
inner	['inə]	a.	内部的，里面的
innovation	[,inə'veiʃən]	n.	革新，创新
inside	['in'said]	a.	内部的；里面的；内侧的
inspector	[in'spektə]	n.	检查员；视察员；巡视员；检验员
instruction	[in'strʌkʃən]	n.	用法说明，操作指南；吩咐，命令
insulation	[,insə'leiʃən]	n.	隔离，隔绝；绝缘；隔热
insurance	[in'ʃuərəns]	n.	保险，保险费
integral	['intigrəl]	a.	构成整体所必需的；完整的
interchangeable	[,intə'tʃeindʒəbl]	a.	可交换的，可互换的，可交替的
intuition	[,intju'iʃən]	n.	直觉
investigate	[in'vestigeit]	vt.	调查，调查研究
It follows that			因此，所以，必然是
item	['aitəm]	n.	条款，节；名称；物品，零件，设备
job site			工地，施工现场
joint	[dʒɔint]	n. a.	接头，接缝；接合点 共同的，联合的
just as			正像，正如
kiln	[kiln]	n.	（用来烧或烘干砖等的）窑，炉
knack	[næk]	n.	技巧；诀窍
knight	[nait]	n.	（中古时代的）武士，骑士
knocker	['nɔkə]	n.	门环
landfill	['lændfil]	n.	垃圾填埋；垃圾填埋地
landscape	['lændskeip]	n.	风景，景色

landscape architect		园林技师
last [lɑːst]	vi.	持续，延续
layer ['leiə]	n.	层，层次
layout ['leiaut]	n.	布局；计划；设计；方案
lead to		导致，引起
lease [liːs]	n.	租约，租契
legion ['liːdʒən]	n.	古罗马军团
legitimate [li'dʒitimət]	a.	法定的；合法的；正当的；合理的
liability [ˌlaiə'biliti]	n.	责任
license ['laisəns]	n.	许可证，执照，牌照
lime [laim]	n.	石灰
lintel ['lintl]	n.	楣，过梁
list [list]	n.	一览表；清单
listed building		注册的文物保护建筑物
literally ['litərəli]	ad.	逐字地；照字面地
load-bearing ['ləud'bɛəriŋ]	a.	承重的
local ['ləukəl]	a.	地方的；本地的
lumber ['lʌmbə]	n.	木材；成材
main house		正房
maintenance ['meintinəns]	n.	维持；维护；保养；维修
manual ['mænjuəl]	a.	用手的，手工的
mapping ['mæpiŋ]	n.	绘制地图，制图，绘图
masonry ['meisənriː]	n.	砖石建筑，砌石工程
mass [mæs]	n.	团，块，堆

New Words and Expressions — Vocabulary

mass wall		实体墙
massing ['mæsiŋ]	n.	块化，密集，集中
maximum ['mæksiməm]	n. a.	最大的量、体积、强度等 最大值的，最大量的
measurement ['meʒəmənt]	n.	衡量，测量；尺寸，大小
mechanics [mi'kæniks]	n.	力学；机械学
mechanize ['mekənaiz]	vt. & vi.	使（过程、工厂等）机械化
medium ['mi:djəm]	n.	媒介；手段，方法，工具
membrane ['membrein]	n.	薄膜，振动片，表层
methane ['meθein]	n.	沼气，甲烷
mineral ['minərəl]	n. & a.	矿物；矿石；矿物质；矿物的，矿质的
minimum ['miniməm]	a. n.	最低的，最小的 最低限度，最小量
mining ['mainiŋ]	n.	采矿（业）
model ['mɔdəl]	n.	模型；设计；型号
monastery ['mɔnəstəri]	n.	修道院
monitor ['mɔnitə]	vt.	监测，检测；监听，监视
monolithic [,mɔnə'liθik]	a.	整体的
mortar ['mɔ:tə]	n.	砂浆，灰浆；房产
mosque ['mɔsk]	n.	清真寺，伊斯兰教寺院
motivation [,məutə'veiʃən]	n.	动机；目的
motorize ['məutəraiz]	vt.	使机动化
mould [məuld]	n. vt.	铸模，模型 用模子做，浇铸
mount [maunt]	n.	安装，装配

mud [mʌd]	n.	泥
mundane [mʌn'dein]	a.	平凡的；平淡的
natural landscape		自然景观
net profit		纯利润
non-structural ['nɔn'strʌktʃərəl]	a.	非结构的
Notre Dame Cathedral in Paris		巴黎圣母院
numerical [njuː'merikəl]	a.	数字的，用数字表示的，数值的
objective [əb'dʒektiv]	n.	目标，目的
occupancy ['ɔkjupənsi]	n.	占有，使用
omission [əu'miʃn]	n.	遗漏；省略
on behalf of		代表
on schedule		按照预定时间，按时间表，准时
opening ['əupəniŋ]	n.	洞；缺口
opposite house		倒座房
ore [ɔː]	n.	矿，矿石
organism ['ɔːɡənizəm]	n.	有机物，有机体；生物；有机体系
orientation [ˌɔːrien'teiʃn]	n.	方向，目标
original [ə'ridʒənəl]	a.	原始的；最初的；原先的
ornament ['ɔːnəmənt]	n.	装饰，点缀；装饰品，点缀品
overlap [ˌəuvə'læp]	n.	重叠的部分
	vt. & vi.	部分重叠
overnight [ˌəuvə'nait]	ad.	突然；很快
oversee [ˌəuvə'siː]	vt.	监督，监视
owner ['əunə]	n.	物主；业主

New Words and Expressions

panel ['pænəl]	n.	护墙板，镶板
participant [pɑː'tisipənt]	n.	参加者，参与者
particular [pə'tikjulə]	a.	个别的；特别的；特殊的
	n.	信息；细节；事项
partition [pɑː'tiʃən]	n.	分隔物，隔墙
party wall		界墙；共用墙
passionate ['pæʃənit]	a.	充满激情的；热切的，强烈的
pathways		廊
pavement ['peivmənt]	n.	铺过的道路，人行道
paycheck ['peitʃek]	n.	薪水支票，工资
payload ['pei,ləud]	n.	载荷，装载量
phase [feiz]	n.	阶段，时期
pier [piə]	n.	柱子，桥墩，墙墩
pile [pail]	n.	桩，堆
pipeline ['paip,lain]	n.	导管，输油管
placement ['pleismənt]	n.	放置，布置
plaster ['plɑːstə]	n.	灰泥，石膏
platform ['plæt,fɔm]	n.	平台，台
plinth [plinθ]	n.	底座，基座
plumb [plʌm]	vt.	用铅垂线测
pluralistic [,pluərə'listik]	a.	多元的；兼职的，兼任的
plywood ['plai,wud]	n.	胶合板，合板，夹板
point [pɔint]	n.	点；尖端；要点；目标；分数；特点
polyethylene [,pɔli'eθiliːn]	n.	聚乙烯

position	[pəˈziʃən]	vt.	安置；定位
pour	[pɔː]	n.	浇注，浇铸
pozzolana	[ˌpɔtsəˈlaːnə]	n.	火山灰（可用作水泥原料）
precipitation	[priˌsipiˈteiʃən]	n.	（雨等）降落；某地区降雨等的量
preliminary	[priˈliminəri]	a.	初步的，预备的，开端的
premises	[ˈpremisiz]	n.	（包括附属建筑、土地等在内的）房屋或其他建筑物
premium	[ˈpriːmiəm]	n.	奖；奖金；额外费用；保险费
preservation	[prezəˈveiʃən]	n.	保护；维护；保存；保留；保持
presumably	[priˈzjuːməbli]	ad.	大概，可能，据推测
prevailing wind direction			盛行风向
primary	[ˈpraiməri]	a.	首要的；主要的；基本的；最初的
prime	[praim]	a.	首要的；主要的；基本的
prime contractor			总承包人
principle	[ˈprinsəpl]	n.	原则，原理；准则，规范
priority	[praiˈɔriti]	n.	重点；优先考虑的事
proactive	[prəuˈæktiv]	a.	有前瞻性的；先发制人的；先行一步的；积极的
procedure	[prəˈsiːdʒə]	n.	步骤；程序；工艺规程，生产过程
procurement	[prəˈkjuəmənt]	n.	获得；采购
professional	[prəˈfeʃənəl]	a.	职业的，专业的；内行的，有经验的
profile	[ˈprəufail]	n.	纵断面，纵剖面图
profit	[ˈprɔfit]	n.	收益，利润；赢利
profitability	[ˌprɔfitəˈbiləti]	n.	盈利性

prone [prəun]	a.	易于……的；很可能……的；有……倾向的	
prone to		易于某事物；很可能做某事	
property [ˈprɔpəti]	n.	财产；资产；特性，性能，属性	
proportion [prəˈpɔːʃən]	n.	均衡；协调；比例	
propose [prəˈpəuz]	vt.	提议；提名，推荐；打算，计划	
proposition [ˌprɔpəˈziʃən]	n.	论点；主张；建议；提案	
purchase [ˈpəːtʃəs]	vt. & n.	买，购买	
pursue [pəˈsjuː]	vt.	追寻；追求；从事；进行	
pyramid [ˈpirəmid]	n.	金字塔；椎体	
quadrangle [ˈkwɔdræŋgl]	n.	四边形，四方院子	
qualification [ˌkwɔlifiˈkeiʃən]	n.	资格；资历	
quantify [ˈkwɔntiˌfai]	vt.	确定……的数量，量化	
rate [reit]	vt.	评定；评价	
ratio [ˈreiʃiəu]	n.	比，比率	
raw material		原材料	
raw [rɔː]	a.	未加工的，处于自然状态的；生的	
ready-mix [ˈrediˈmiks]	a.	掺水即可用的	
rear [riə]	n.	后部；后面；背后	
refinement [riˈfainmənt]	n.	精炼的产品，精细的改进	
regionalism [ˈriːdʒənəˌlizəm]	n.	地方主义，乡土主义，乡土色彩	
regulation [ˌregjuˈleiʃən]	n.	规章，规则；管理，控制，调节	
reinforced concrete		钢筋混凝土	
relatively [ˈrelətivli]	ad.	相对地；相比较而言	

relevant ['reləvənt]	a.	有关的；切题的
renewable [ri'njuəbl]	a.	可更新的，可恢复的，可继续的
reposition [ri:pə'ziʃən]	vt.	调换位置
reservoir ['rezəvwɑ:]	n.	水库；储藏；汇集
resistant [ri'zistənt]	a.	有抵抗力的，抵抗的
resolved [ri'zɔlvd]	a.	下定决心的，断然的
rest with		是……的责任
retrofit ['retrəfit]	vt.	更新；改进；改型；改造
ridge [ridʒ]	vi.	成脊状
rip [rip]	vt.	锯开，割裂
roadway ['rəudwei]	n.	车行道，道路
rot [rɔt]	vi.	腐烂；腐坏
rug [rʌg]	n.	地毯；壁毯
run over		超过
runway ['rʌnwei]	n.	(机场的)跑道；(停车场的)车道，通道
rustic ['rʌstik]	a.	粗面石工的；用粗糙的木材或树枝制作的
sanitary ['sænitəri]	a.	清洁的，卫生的，保健的
scale [skeil]	n.	规模；等级；刻度，标度；比例尺
scarify ['skɛərifai]	vt.	切割；软化
schedule ['skedʒul]	n.	进度表；预定计划表；清单，明细表
scheduling ['skedʒuliŋ]	n.	时序安排，行程安排
schematic [ski:'mætik]	a.	图表的；图解的
scope [skəup]	n.	范围；余地，机会
scraper ['skreipə]	n.	刮刀；平土机；铲土机

screed	[skri:d]	n.	(定墙上灰泥厚薄的)准条；匀泥尺，样板
screen wall			影壁
seasoned	['si:zənd]	a.	成熟的；老练的
secluded	[si'klu:did]	a.	与世隔绝的，隐退的，隐居的
secondary	['sekəndəri]	a.	次要的，次等的
section	['sekʃən]	n.	断面，剖面，断面图；拆；段；部分
sector	['sektə]	n.	部门；领域
secure	[si'kjuə]	a.	安全的，无危险的，牢固的；稳当的；牢靠的
segment	['segmənt]	n.	部分，片段
sentiment	['sentimənt]	n.	温情；伤感；观点，主意
serve as			被用作……，充当……，起……的作用
settlement	['setlmənt]	n.	沉陷；沉积物；沉淀，下沉，沉积
shaft	[ʃa:ft]	n.	井状通道；通风井；(电梯的)升降机井
shared	[ʃɜəd]	a.	共享的，共用的
shear	[ʃiə]	n.	剪切，剪力
shed	[ʃed]	n.	棚，库
shoring	['ʃɔ:riŋ]	n.	利用支柱的支撑，支柱
shrine	[ʃrain]	n.	圣地，圣坛，神圣场所
side houses			厢房
sign	[sain]	n.	标记，符号；标志；迹象
siheyuan			四合院
silo	['sailəu]	n.	筒仓
simultaneously	[saiməl'teiniəsli]	ad.	同时，一起

single	['siŋgl]	a.	单一的；单个的
site	[sait]	n.	地点，位置；工地
skeleton	['skelitn]	n.	骨架；框架
sketch	[sketʃ]	n.	简图，草图
skyscraper	['skai,skreipə]	n.	摩天大楼
solar	['səulə]	a.	太阳的，日光的
solid	['sɔlid]	a.	结实的，稳定的，坚固的
sound	[saund]	a.	完好的；健康的；健全的；无损伤的
span	[spæn]	vt.	(桥、拱等)横跨，跨越
		n.	跨距；跨度
spatial	['speiʃəl]	a.	空间的，立体空间的，三维空间的
specialized	['speʃəlaizd]	a.	专门的；专用的；专科的
specific	[spi'sifik]	a.	特定的；具体的；确切的
specification	[,spesifi'keiʃən]	n.	规格；规格说明；规范；详细说明
specify	['spesifai]	vt.	具体指定；详细指明；明确说明
spectator	['spekteiə]	n.	观众，旁观者
spontaneity	[,spɔntə'ni:iti]	n.	自发性，自动
square	[skwɛə]	n.	正方形
stability	[stə'biliti]	n.	稳定；稳定性，稳定度
stack	[stæk]	n.	堆，垛，大量，一大堆
		vt. & vi.	堆积
standard	['stændəd]	n.	标准，水准；规范，规格
standpoint	['stændpɔint]	n.	立场；观点
stationary	['steiʃənəri]	a.	不动的，固定的

英文	音标	词性	中文
steel	[stiːl]	n.	钢
stepping-stone	['stepiŋˌstəun]	n.	踏脚石；方法，手段
stiffness	['stifnis]	n.	硬挺度，抗挠性
stimulate	['stimjuleit]	vt.	刺激；激励；激发
stormwater	[stɔːm'wɔːtə]	n.	暴雨水
strategy	['strætidʒi]	n.	战略，策略
stratify	['strætifai]	vt.	（使）分层，成层
stretcher	['stretʃə]	n.	顺砌砖；横砌石
string	[striŋ]	n.	线，细绳
strip	[strip]	n.	条状，带状
structural	['strʌktʃərəl]	a.	结构的，建筑的，构造的
stylish	['stailiʃ]	a.	有风度的，有气派的，有格调的
stylistic	[stai'listik]	a.	风格上的
subcontractor	[ˌsʌbkən'træktə]	n.	分包商
submit	[səb'mit]	vt.	呈送，提交
substance	['sʌbstəns]	n.	物质
substitute	['sʌbstitjuːt]	n.	代用品，代替者，代替物
		vt. & vi.	代替，替换，代用
subterranean	[ˌsʌbtə'reiniən]	a.	地表下面的；地下的
subvert	[sʌb'vəːt]	vt.	颠覆，破坏（政治制度、宗教信仰等）
such that			到这样的程度
sunken	['sʌŋkən]	a.	低于周围平面的，凹陷的；下陷的
superintendent	[ˌsjuːpərin'tendənt]	n.	管理员，指挥人，总段长
superstition	[ˌsjuːpə'stiʃən]	n.	迷信，迷信行为

survey [sə'vei]	vt.	测量；调查；观察
surveyor [sə'veiə]	n.	测量员
suspend [sə'spend]	vt.	悬，挂，吊
sustain [sə'sten]	vt.	保持；供养，维持；支持；经受
sustainable [sə'steinəbl]	a.	可持续的
synchronic [siŋ'krɔnik]	a.	同时期的，同时发生的
take advantage of		利用，运用
take sth. into account		计及；斟酌；体谅；考虑
tangible ['tændʒəbəl]	a.	明确的；确切的；真实的；可触知的
tarpaulin [tɑː'pɔːlin]	n.	防水帆布，防水帆布罩
tedious ['tiːdiəs]	a.	令人厌倦的；烦人的
tell-tale		位移指示器
temporary ['tempərəri]	a.	临时的，暂时的，短时间的
tendency ['tendənsi]	n.	倾向，趋势
tension ['tenʃən]	n.	张力，拉力；拉紧，绷紧
termination [tɜːmi'neiʃən]	n.	终点；结局；终止
terrain [tə'rein]	n.	地形；地貌；地势；地带
testament ['testəmənt]	n.	证明，证据
texture ['tekstʃə]	n.	（材料等的）构造；（岩石等的）纹理
the eight diagrams of divination		八卦占卜
the five elements		（金木水火土）五行
thereafter [ðɛər'ɑːftə]	ad.	之后，以后
thermal ['θɜːməl]	a.	热的，热量的，由热造成的
thinking ['θiŋkiŋ]	n.	思想，思考；想法；意见；见解

New Words and Expressions · Vocabulary

third-party		第三方；第三当事人
thrive [θraiv]	vi.	茁壮成长；蓬勃发展；繁荣
timber ['timbə]	n.	木材，木料
tipping load		倾覆载荷
to some degree		在某种程度上
tonnage ['tʌnidʒ]	n.	吨位，总吨数，船舶吨位
topographical [ˌtɔpə'græfikəl]	n.	地志的；地形学的
topography [tə'pɔgrəfi]	n.	地形，地貌，地势；地形学；地形测量学
topsoil ['tɔpˌsɔil]	n.	表层土
tow [təu]	vt.	拖，拉，拽
toxic ['tɔksik]	a.	有毒的；中毒的
tranquility [træŋ'kwiliti]	n.	宁静
transcend [træn'send]	vt.	超出或超越
trencher ['trentʃə]	n.	挖沟机
trigger ['trigə]	vt.	引发，引起
trowel ['trauəl]	n.	泥刀，抹子，小铲子
tunnel ['tʌnəl]	n.	隧道，地道
tunneler ['tʌnələ]	n.	隧道掘进机
turbine ['tə:bin]	n.	涡轮机；透平机
underground ['ʌndəgraund]	a. ad.	地下的；地下组织的；秘密的 在地下；秘密地
undisturbed earth		坚硬泥土
uniform ['ju:nifɔ:m]	a.	全都相同的，一律的，清一色的
uniformly ['ju:nifɔ:mli]	ad.	一致地；均匀地

unremitting [ˌʌnri'mitiŋ]		a.	不放松的；不停止的；不间断的；坚持的
up to			（数量上）多达
urban ['ə:bən]		a.	城市的
utility [ju:'tiliti]		n.	有用；实用；效用；[pl.] 公用设施
utilize ['ju:tilaiz]		vt.	利用，使用
variable ['vɛəriəbl]		n.	可变因素；变数
		a.	变化的，可变的，易变的
vary ['vɛəri]		vi.	改变，变动，变化
vault [vɔ:lt]		n.	柱，圆柱
veneer [vi'niə]		vt.	在（某物表面）上加薄片镶饰
ventilation [ˌventi'leiʃən]		n.	空气流通，通风设备；通风方法
veranda [və'rændə]		n.	阳台；游廊；走廊
verandah [və'rændə]		n.	阳台；走廊
verbal ['və:bəl]		a.	口头的，词语的，言语的，字句的
vermilion [və'miljən]		n.	朱红色；鲜红色
		a.	朱红色的；鲜红色的
versatile ['və:sətail]		a.	（指工具、机器等）多用途的，多功能的
vertical ['və:tikəl]		a.	垂直的，竖的，直立的
villa ['vilə]		n.	别墅，公馆
virtual ['və:tjuəl]		a.	实质上的，事实上的，实际上的
visualize ['viʒuəlaiz]		vt.	设想，想象
vital ['vaitəl]		a.	极重要的，必不可少的
void [vɔid]		a.	空的，空虚的
waterproof ['wɔ:təpru:f]		a.	不透水的，防水的
		vt.	使防水；使不透水

New Words and Expressions · Vocabulary

wear and tear		损坏，损耗，用坏
weather ['weðə]	v.	晒干；风化
wetland ['wetlænd]	n.	湿地；沼地
when it comes to		当涉及；当谈到
with respect to		涉及、提到或关于某事物；在……方面
worship ['wə:ʃip]	vi.	做礼拜
	vt.	崇拜
zoning ['zəuniŋ]	n.	分区；分区制

附录 I 科技论文的写作格式及规范

一篇完整的科技论文一般包括以下 9 个部分：题名、署名、摘要、关键词、引言、正文、结论、致谢和参考文献。

1. 题名(Title，Topic)

题名又叫题目、文题、标题，是科技论文的中心和总纲。题目要紧扣论文内容，或论文内容与论文题目要互相匹配、紧扣，即题要扣文，文也要扣题，这是撰写论文的基本准则。题名一般不超过 20 个汉字，必要时可加副题名，使标题既充实、准确又不流于笼统和一般化。应避免使用非公知公用的缩写词、字符、代号，尽量不出现数学式和化学式。

2. 署名(Name)

署名是指在论文主题内容的构思，具体研究工作的执行，以及撰稿执笔等方面的全部或局部上作出主要贡献的人员，能够对论文的主要内容负责答辩的人员，是论文的法定权人和责任者。作者署名放于题名下方，团体作者的执笔人也可注于首页页脚或文末。署名包括工作单位及联系方式。工作单位应写全称，并包括所在城市名称及邮政编码。有时为进行文献分析，要求作者提供性别、出生年月、职务职称、电话号码、电子邮箱等信息。

3. 摘要(Abstract)

摘要是对论文的内容不加注释和评论的简短陈述，是文章内容的高度概括。一般论文摘要位于题名和正文之间，一般不分段，根据篇幅大小一般限制其摘要字数不超过论文字数的5%。例如：对于一篇6000字的论文，其摘要一般不超出300字。其主要内容包括：①该项研究工作的目的及其重要性。②研究的主要内容，指明完成了哪些工作。③获得的基本结论和研究成果，突出作者的新见解。④结论或结果的意义。

4. 关键词(Keywords)

关键词是为了满足文献标引或检索工作的需要而从论文中萃取出的，表示全文主题内容信息条目的单词、词组或术语，一般列出3~5个。关键词的一般选择方法是：由作者在完成论文写作后，纵观全文，选出能表示论文主要内容的信息或词汇，这些信息或词汇，也可以从论文标题或论文内容中去找。关键词选得是否恰当，关系到该文被检索和该成果的利用率。

5. 引言(Introduction)

引言又称前言、导言、序言、绪论，属于整篇论文的引论部分，它是一篇科技论文的开场白，由它引出文章，所以写在正文之前。引言的内容包括：说明本研究工作的缘起、背景、目的、意义等；介绍与本研究相关领域前人研究的历史、现状、成果评价及其相互关系；陈述本项研究的宗旨，包括研究目的、理论依据、方案设计、要解决的问题等。引言应言简意赅，不可与摘要雷同，或成为摘要的注释。学术论文的引言根据论文篇幅的大小和内容的多少而定，一般为200~600字，短则可不足100字，长则可达1000字左右。写作过程应按逻辑顺序，做到文理贯通，条理清晰。

6. 正文(Maintext)

正文是科技论文的主体，是用论据经过论证证明论点而表述科研成果的核心部分。正文占论文的主要篇幅，可以包括以下部分或内容：调查对象、基本原理、实验和观测方法、仪器设备、材料原料、实验和观测结果、计算方法和编程原理、数据资料、经过加工整理的图表、形成的论点和导出的结论等。其写作要求如下。

(1)理论性论文。用理论分析或计算分析来证明论文观点的正确。对于研究对象进行精确的描述，定量地揭示各因素之间的关系，在写作方法上，常用举例、推理、反证、类比、对比、因果分析、归谬法等。在写作要求上，应论点明确而唯一，论据充分而必要，层次清楚，结构合理，逻辑性强。

(2)实验性论文。实验是为科学上实现新的发现的一种手段。其论文的内容一般包括理论分析，实验材料、方法，实验结果及分析等几部分。在论述实验材料和方法部分，要把材料的来源、性质和数量，实验使用的仪器、设备、实验条件和测试方法交代清楚，其目的是使别人能重复操作进行同样的实验，以验证新发现的正确性和可靠性。

(3) 试验性论文。试验是相对技术而言、为解决或验证技术措施的可行性服务的。写作的内容一般包括试验的目的，即要解决或验证的问题，试验的方法、试验结果及分析等。

(4) 创新性技术论文。以自然理论为基础，应用自然科学的最新成果实现技术创新，或者运用已有的科学技术理论和自己的实践经验实现技术创新而形成的论文(此类论文较为多见)。例文：《灰色系统理论在旱灾分析中的应用》。

7. 结论 (Conclusion)

科技论文一般在正文后面要有结论。结论是将实验和观测得到的数据、结果，经过判断、推理、归纳等逻辑分析，而得到的对事物的本质和规律的认识，是整篇论文的总论点。读者阅读论文的习惯一般是首先看题名，其次是看摘要，再次看结论。结论的内容主要包括：研究结果说明了什么问题，得出了什么规律，解决了什么实际问题或理论问题；对前人的研究成果作了哪些补充、修改和证实，有什么创新；本文研究工作的领域内还有哪些尚待解决的问题，以及解决这些问题的基本思路和关键。结论应做到准确、完整、明确、精练，用语斩钉截铁，数据准确可靠，不能含糊其辞，模棱两可。文字上也不应夸大，对尚不能完全肯定的内容，注意留有余地。

8. 致谢 (Acknowledgements)

致谢位于正文后，参考文献前。现代科学技术研究往往不是一个人能单独完成的，而需要他人的合作与帮助，因此，当研究成果以论文形式发表时，作者应当对他人的劳动给以充分肯定，并对他们表示感谢。致谢的对象是：凡对本研究直接提供过资金、设备、人力，以及文献资料等支持和帮助的团体和个人。编写致谢时不要直书其名，应加上"某教授"、"某博士"等敬称。如："本研究得到'XXX 教授，XXX 博士'的帮助，谨致谢意"，"试验工作是 XXX 单位完成的，XXX 工程师、XXX 师傅承担了大量试验，对他们谨致谢意"。

9. 参考文献 (References)

在科技论文中，凡是引用前人(包括作者自己过去)已发表的文献中的观点、数据和材料等，都要对它们在文中出现的地方予以标明，并在文末(致谢段之后)列出参考文献表。这项工作叫做参考文献著录。参考文献的著录格式如下。

1) 专著著录格式

［序号］著者．书名［M］．版本(第一版不写)．出版地：出版者，出版年：起止页码．

例：［1］孙家广，杨长青．计算机图形学［M］．北京：清华大学出版社，1995：26—28.

2) 期刊著录格式

［序号］作者．题名［J］．刊名，出版年份，卷号(期号)：起止页码．

例：［2］李旭东，宗光华，毕树生，等．生物工程微操作机器人视觉系统的研究［J］．北京航空航天大学学报，2002，28(3)：249—252.

3) 论文集著录格式

［序号］作者．题名［C］//主编．论文集名．出版地：出版者，出版年：起止页码．

例：［3］张佐光，张晓宏，仲伟虹，等．多相混杂纤维复合材料拉伸行为分析［C］//张为民．第九届全国复合材料学术会议论文集(下册)．北京：世界图书出版公司，1996：410—416.

4) 学位论文著录格式

［序号］作者．题名［D］．保存地点：保存单位，年．

例：［4］金宏．导航系统的精度及容错性能的研究［D］．北京：北京航空航天大学自动控制系，1998.

5) 科技报告著录格式

［序号］作者．题名［R］．编号，出版年．

例：［5］Kyungmoon Nho. Automatic landing system design using fuzzy logic［R］. AIAA－98－4484，1998.

6) 国际或国家标准著录格式

［序号］标准编号，标准名称［S］．

例：［6］GB/T 16159—1996，汉语拼音正词法基本规则［S］．

7) 专利著录格式

［序号］专利所有者．专利题名：专利国别，专利号［P］．公告日期或公开日期．

例：［7］姜锡洲．一种温热外敷药制备方案：中国，881056073［P］．1989－07－06.

8) 电子文献著录格式

［序号］作者．题名［文献类型标志/文献载体标志］．出版地：出版者，出版年(更新或修改日期)［引用日期］．获取和访问路径．

例：［8］Pacs－l：the public－access computer systems forum［EB/OL］. Houston, Tex：University of Houston Libraries，1989［1995－05－17］. http://info.lib.uh.edu/pacs1.html.

表 1　文献类型和标志代码

文献类型	标志代码
普通图书	M
会议录	C
汇编	G
报纸	N
期刊	J
学位论文	D
报告	R
标准	S
专利	P
数据库	DB
计算机程序	CP
电子公告	EB

附录 Ⅱ 科技英语的翻译

科技英语(English for Science and Technology, EST)是英语的一种语体，有关自然科学和社会科学的学术著作、论文、研究报告、专利产品的说明等均属此类。科技英语注重科学性、逻辑性、正确性与严密性，在词汇、语法、修饰方面具有自己的特色。因此，在进行科技英语翻译时必须了解科技英语的语言结构特点，以便于有意识地选择适当的翻译方法与技巧来处理科技英语文章。

一、科技英语的语言结构特点

1. 大量使用被动语态

被动语态在普通英语中是最基本的语法，简单易学。科技英语中大量使用被动语态，不是为了追求文章语言的艺术美，而是为了讲求叙述文章的客观，语言简洁，结构严谨，和普通英语文章有着显著不同，加深读者对所叙述事物的深刻印象，摒弃不必要的东西。

例如：This procedure is generally called "mapping" because the description is often provided by way of a site map.

这一步骤一般称作"制图"，因为这种描述通常是通过施工图来实现的。

Nowadays most buildings are made more than one storey high.

当今的大多数建筑物都是多层的。

2. 大量使用名词化结构

科技英语在科技文体中随着科学技术的发展形成一种实用正式的文体，它的名词化倾向越来越突出。翻译时可以看出它是由及物动词加 -ment，-tion，-sion，-ence 等后缀派生的名词。这样的表达可以语言简洁、行文自然、造句灵活、叙述准确、表达客观，符合科技文体的要求。

例如：The final appearance of the building depends very much on its finishing.

建筑物的最后外观很大程度上取决于精整装饰。

The provision of a plinth beam and damp-proof course at plinth level are very important in building construction.

在建筑物建造中，基柱梁的作用以及基柱的防潮构件是非常重要的。

3. 频繁使用非谓语动词

在科技英语中使用非谓语动词结构可以更好、更准确地描述各个事物之间的关系，事物的位置和状态的变化。

例如：Moreover, concrete usually provides stiffness for structures to keep them stable.

另外，混泥土用来固定建筑物结构以保持其稳固。

A civil engineer's duties on a project vary depending on the particular discipline.

学科不同，土木工程师的职责也有所不同。

4. 大量使用复合词与缩略词

大量使用复合词与缩略词是科技文章的特点之一，复合词从过去的双词组合发展到多词组合；缩略词趋向于任意构词。

例如：load-bearing　　　承重的（双词合成形容词）

high-speed　　　　高速的（双词合成形容词）

drywall　　　　　　干砌墙壁（无连字符复合词）

waterproof　　　　防水的（无连字符复合词）

GPS（Global Position System）全球定位系统（缩略词）

IQ（Intelligence Quotient）智商（缩略词）

MAX（Maximum）最大的、最大限度的（缩略词）

lab（laboratory）实验室（缩略词）

mm（Millimeter）毫米（缩略词）

5. 经常出现长句、难句

为了表述一个复杂概念，使之逻辑严密，结构紧凑，科技文章中往往出现许多长句。

例如：In building construction, we study how the civil works are carried out the field after they have been planned by an architect and structurally designed by an engineer.

在房屋建筑中要研究的是，建筑工程在由建筑师完成平面设计并由工程师完成结构设计后，如何执行场地施工。

Some of the stylistic distinctions found in these diverse aesthetic realities reflect profound differences in design values and thinking, but this is not the case for all stylistic distinctions, as some stylistic distinctions builds on similar thinking and values.

美学现实中的一些风格差异也反映了设计观和设计思想的截然不同，但是，对于所有的风格，情况并非如此，因为一些风格差异是以相似的思想和价值观为基础。

二、科技英语的翻译技巧

1. 长句翻译

分析科技英语长句时一般可以采用下面的方法。

(1) 找出全句的主语、谓语和宾语，从整体上把握句子的结构。

(2) 找出句中所有的谓语结构、非谓语动词、介词短语和从句的引导词。

(3) 分析从句和短语的功能，如：是否为主语从句、宾语从句、表语从句等。若是状语从句，它是表示时间、原因、结果，还是表示条件，等等。

(4) 分析词、短语和从句之间的相互关系，如：定语从句所修饰的先行词是哪一个，等等。

(5) 注意插入语等其他成分。

(6) 注意分析句子中是否有固定词组或固定搭配。

例如：Even when we turn off the bedside lamp and are fast asleep, electricity is still working for us, driving our refrigerators, heating our water or keeping our rooms air-conditioned.

即使在人们关掉了床头灯深深地进入梦乡时，电仍在为人们工作：为电冰箱提供动力，把水加热，或使室内空调机继续运转。

分析：这是一个时间状语从句，由关系副词"when"引导。主句中的3个现在分词短语"driving our refrigerators, heating our water or keeping our rooms air-conditioned"在句中均作伴随状语，修饰谓语动词"is still working"，在英语长句的翻译过程中常用的具体方法有下列4种。

1) 顺序法

顺序翻译法是经常使用，也是最便利的翻译方法，就是指基本上按英语句子的语序把英语长句"化整为零"，即在英语原句的连接处，如使用关联词语处、并列或转接处、后续成分与主体连接处等，以及按意群将英语的长句断开翻译成若干汉语分句。

例如：But now it is realized that supplies of some of them are limited, and it is even possible to give a reasonable estimate of their "expectation of life", the time it will take to exhaust all known sources and reserves of these materials.

可是现在人们意识到，其中有些矿物质的蕴藏量是有限的，人们甚至还可以比较合理地估计出这些矿物质"可望存在多少年"，也就是说，经过若干年后，这些矿物的全部已知矿源和储量将消耗殆尽。

2）逆序法

逆序翻译法是将英语长句中所传达的信息在译文中分割成若干短句，然后再按照汉语习惯表达法进行重新安排，很多时候，汉语译文中各分句的顺序同原文中信息铺陈的顺序恰好相反，比如汉语复合句中往往将主要信息后置（少数情况除外），而英语复合句则往往将主要信息前置，次要信息后置。也就是说，将英语句子信息前重心移向汉语句子后重心的翻译方法，往往称为逆序翻译法。

例如：A material which has the property of elasticity will return to its original size and shape when the forces producing strain are removed.

如果把产生应变的力去掉，具有弹性的材料就会恢复到它原来的体积和形状。

3）拆分法

英语的长句可以盘根错节，从句套从句，但在汉语中行文方式同英语的行文方式却不尽相同。因此，在将英语的长句翻译成汉语时，应根据汉语的地道方式进行适度调整。调整的方式之一就是根据英语原文，按照层次将原文所表达的意思在汉语中用不同的句子表达出来。可以将原文中的单个词或词组扩成句子，或者将一个句子拆开为两个以上的单句，即将句子成分前后加上的某些修饰语（如定语、状语、定语从句、状语从句）、多级短语、多级从句等翻译成句子。

例如：All they have to do is to press a button, and they can see plays, films, operas and shows of every kind, not to mention political discussions and the latest exciting football match.

他们所必须做的只是按一下开关。开关一开，就可以看到电视剧、电影、歌剧，以及其他各种各样的文艺节目。至于政治问题的辩论、最近的激动人心的足球赛更是不在话下。

4）合句法

有时候，为了符合英语叙述习惯，达到确切表达原意的目的，可以把几个内容相关的汉语小句或片段合译成一个英语简单句或复合句。

例如：Modern scientific and technical books, especially textbooks, require revision at short intervals if their authors wish to keep pace with new ideas, observations and discoveries.

对于现代科技书籍，特别是对于教科书来说，要是作者希望自己书中的内容能与新概念、新观察到的事实和新发现同步发展，那么就需要每隔较短的时间，将书中的内容重新修订。

2. 被动语态的译法

1）将英语的被动句翻译为汉语的主动句式

例如：A new way of displaying time has been given by electronics.

电子技术提供了一种新的显示时间的方法。

Silver is known to be better than copper in conductivity.

大家知道，银的导电性比铜好。

2）把英语的被动句翻译成汉语的被动句

例如：Over the years, tool and technology themselves as a source of fundamental innovation have largely been ignored by historians and philosophers of science.

工具和技术本身作为根本性创新的源泉，多年来很大程度上被科学史学家和哲学家们忽视了。

Concrete is made of cement, sand, stones and water.

混凝土是用水泥、沙子、石子和水制成的。

3. 词义引申

词义引申是指改变原文字面意思的翻译方法。翻译时，有时会碰到某些词在词典上找不到适当的词义，如任意硬套或逐词死译，译文则会生硬晦涩，难以确切表达原意，甚至造成误解。所以，应根据上下文和逻辑关系，从其基本含义出发，进一步加以引申，选择适当的词来表达。

例如：Perhaps the only trouble with copper is that it is not hard enough for some uses.

就某些用途来说，铜的唯一缺点也许是硬度不够。（原文的 trouble 本来是"麻烦"的意思，但是与"铜"联系在一起，就可以引申为"缺点"来翻译了。）

Optics technology is one of the most sensational developments in recent years.

光学技术是近年来轰动一时的科学成就之一。

4. 词量增减

1）词量增加

翻译时，往往遇到一些词句在英语表达上是清楚的，但直译成中文，不是意思不清楚，便是译文不通顺。因此，为了使译文意思明确，或者仅仅为了修辞的目的，需要增加一些原文中无其形而有其义的词。

例如：The propagation of such microwaves will be explained in terms of Maxwell's equations.

这种微波的传播原理要用麦克斯韦方程来解释。（propagation 译为"传播原理"，增加"原理"）

A new kind of aircraft—small, cheap, pilotless—is attracting increasing attention.

一种新型的飞机正越来越引起人们的注意——这种飞机体积小、造价低、无人驾驶。（增加"体积"、"造价"）

2) 词量减少

为了更好地表达原意，翻译时往往可以省略原文中某些词，以使译文更严谨、更精炼、更明确。例如：英语中的冠词、介词、连接词、代词等。而且，在英译汉中词量减少的情况要比增加的情况更为普遍。

例如：The air was removed from between the two pipes.

两根管子之间的空气已抽出。（省略介词 from）

A square has four equal sides.

正方形四边相等。（省略动词 have）

5. 词类转换

为了适应汉语的表达习惯或达到一定的修饰目的，在翻译时可以改变原文中某些词的词性。这类译法叫词类转换。

例如：Were there no friction, transmission of motion would be impossible.

没有摩擦就不能传递运动。

Rockets have found application for the exploration of the universe.

火箭已经用来探索宇宙。

Generally speaking, neither gold nor stones are soluble in water.

一般说来，金子和石头都不能溶解于水。

The lower stretches of rivers show considerable variety.

河下流的情况是多种多样的。

6. 成分转换

句子成分转换是指英语中的某一句子成分译成汉语时转换成另一种句子成分，以达到译文逻辑正确，通顺流畅，重点突出等目的。

例如：The wings are responsible for keeping the air plane in the air.

机翼的用途是使飞机在空中保持不坠。（wings 原为主语，转译为定语）

Gold is similar in colour to brass.

金子的颜色和黄铜相似。（colour 原为状语，转译为主语，而原主语 gold 则译为 colour 的定语）

The proton has considerably more mass than the electron.

质子的质量比电子大得多。

（将 has 的宾语 mass 译为主语，而把 proton 译为 mass 的定语，has 省略不译。）

7. 成分分译

成分分译就是改变原文句子结构的一种译法。即把原文较长的句子成分，或不易安排的句子成分分出来另作处理，一般译成汉语短语或独立语。分译得当可以使译文层次分明，简练明确，合乎汉语规范。

例如：Lower temperature are associated with lower growth rates.（主语分译）

温度一低，生长速率就慢下去。

This was thought likely to happen in the late 1860s.（谓语分译）

人们很可能认为，这发生在 19 世纪 60 年代后期。

Pig iron is an alloy of iron and carbon with carbon content more than 2 percent.（定语分译）

生铁是一种铁碳合金，其含碳量在百分之二以上。

Heat is required to change ice to water.（状语分译）

冰变为水，就需要热。

8. 反面着笔

反面着笔是指翻译时突破原文的形式，采用变换语气的办法处理词句，把肯定的译成否定的，或把否定的译成肯定的，以使译文流畅、自然，更合乎汉语的习惯。

例如：The bomb missed the target.（肯定译成否定）

炸弹没有击中目标。

It is beyond your right to sign such a contract.（肯定译成否定）

你无权签订这样的合同。

If you need any help, please don't hesitate to tell me.（否定译成肯定）

如果需要帮忙请尽管说。

The device of total station was not much used until 1990s.（否定译成肯定）

直到 20 世纪 90 年代，全站仪才被大量使用。

9. 重复译法

重复译法是指翻译时重复原文中某些词，使译文表达明确具体。由于英汉之间存在差异，有些词在英语句中是不必重复的，但在汉语中却必须重复，否则就会造成文理不通或逻辑混乱。

例如：The chief effects of electric currents are the magnetic, heating and chemical effects.（重复共同部分）

电流的主要效应是磁效应、热效应和化学效应。

Electrical and magnetic quantities are less simple than length, mass or time.（重复共同部分）

电量和磁量不像长度、质量或时间那么简单。

Some metals are easy to machine; others are not.（重复省略部分）

有些金属易于加工；另一些金属却不易加工。

Locomotives are built of steel, and airplanes of aluminium.（重复省略部分）

火车头由钢制成，而飞机由铝制成。

Of all the chemical elements hydrogen is the lightest one.（重复所代名词）

在所有化学元素中，氢是最轻的元素。

Of all the subjects, maths is the one that I am the most interested in.（重复所代名词）

在所有的课程中，数学是我最感兴趣的一门课。

附录 III

建筑工程专业英语词汇

architecture	建筑学
absolute elevation	绝对标高
ancient architecture	古代建筑
angle steel	角钢
annular	环形
anti-corrosion	防腐
architectonics	建筑原理
architectural composition	建筑构图
architectural conception	建筑构思
architectural control	建筑管理
architectural creation	建筑创作
architectural detail	建筑大样

architectural mechanics	建筑力学
architectural metalwork	建筑大五金
architectural physics	建筑物理
architectural scale	建筑尺度
architectural style	建筑风格
architectural treatment	建筑处理
area	面积
arrangement of reinforcement	配筋
as-built drawing	竣工图
assistant engineer	助理工程师
auxiliary buildings	附属建筑
average dimension	平均尺寸
axis	轴线
azimuth	方位角
back elevation	背立面
balcony	阳台
basic data for design	设计基础资料
basic design	基础设计
bay	开间
bearing wall	承重墙
bitumen for building	建筑沥青
brick wall	砖墙

brightness	亮度
building board	建筑板材
building code	建筑规范
building construction	建筑构造
building contractor	建筑承包商
building cost estimate	建筑估价
building elevation	建筑立面
building height	建筑高度
building industry	建筑工业
building machinery	建筑机械
building material testing	建筑材料检验
building model	建筑模型
building orientation	建筑朝向
building regulations	建筑规程
building sheet	建筑钢板
building structure	建筑结构
building subsystem	建筑辅助系统
building trades	建筑工种
building unit	建筑单元
capacity	容量
ceiling board	天花板
cement floor	水泥地面

center line	中心线
centimeter	厘米
chief engineer	总工程师
circle	圆圈
city planning	城市规划
civil	土木
civil architecture	民用建筑
civil engineer	土木工程师
civil engineering	土木工程
clear distance	净距
clear span	净跨
clearance	净空
closed type	封闭式
coding	编号
column grid	柱网
composite panel	复合板
concrete floor	混凝土地面
conduction	传导
cone	圆锥形
constant temperature	恒温
construction cost	建筑费
construction cost estimate	建筑成本预算

construction drawing	施工图
construction work quantity	建筑安装工程量
construction(al) steel	建筑钢
contour line	等高线
convection	对流
coordinate	坐标
cross(transverse) section	横剖面
curves	曲线
damp-proof course(D.P.C)	防潮层
depth	进深
design manager	设计经理
design order	设计任务书
designed elevation	设计标高
detail design	详细设计
detail drawings	详图
detail No.	节点号
detail with enlarged scale	局部放大图
developed dimension	展开尺寸
developed drawing	展开图
dew point	露点
diagram	示意图
dimension line	尺寸线

dot and dash line	点画线
dotted line	虚线
double span	双跨
draftsman	制图员
drain ditch	排水沟
dump-proof	防潮
dust-proof	防尘
earth-work drawing	土方工程图
electric lighting	电气照明
electric power supply	电力供应
electrical engineer	电气工程师
elevation	立面；标高
ellipse	椭圆形
engineering geological data	工程地质资料
expert	专家
extension	扩建
external(exterior)wall	外墙
farm building	农业建筑
feasibility study	可行性研究
filled earth	填土
fire extinguisher	灭火器
fire hydrant	消火栓

fire-prevention	防火
floor drain	地漏
floor elevation	室内地面标高
flow diagram	流程示意图
foot	英尺
force	力
formwork drawing	模板图
freight traffic volume	货流量
front elevation	正立面
front page	首页
gallon	加仑
general specification	总说明
glaze	眩光
grade	地坪；等级
greenbelt	绿地
gross weight	毛重
ground elevation	室外地面标高
gypsum	石膏
H. V. A. C(heating、ventilation and air conditioning)	采暖通风
hatching line	影线
headroom	净高
heat power supply	热力供应

heavy industrial	重工业的
hectare	公顷
hyperbola	双曲线
illumination	照明
inch	英寸
industrial building	工业建筑
information drawing	条件图
inside diameter	内径
instrument	仪表
internal(interior)wall	内墙
kilogram/cubic meter	千克/立方米
kip	千磅
legend	图例
light industrial	轻工业的
list of building materials	建筑材料表
list of contents and description	图纸目录及说明
list of drawings	图纸目录
list of standards and specification adopted	采用标准规范目录
load diagram	荷载简图
longitudinal section	纵剖面
marble	大理石
mass	质量

mechanical engineer	机械工程师
mechanical power	动力
metallic materials	金属材料
meter	米
millimeter	毫米
modern architecture	现代建筑
modular system	模数制
multi-span	多跨
natural lighting	天然采光
net weight	净重
Newton/square meter	牛顿/平方米
noise	噪音
offsite	厂区外
open type	开敞式
original data	原始资料
outside diameter	外径
overall dimension	外形尺寸
overhead pipeline	架空管线
parabola	抛物线
paraboloid	抛物面
parallelogram	平行四边形
passage area	通道面积

pedestrian volume	人流量
percentage	百分比
perspective drawing	透视图
pipe rack	管架
pipeline gallery	管廊
piping	管道
plan	平面图
planning engineer	计划工程师
planning proposals	计划建议书
pound	磅
preliminary design	初步设计
preliminary estimate	概算
principal architect	首席建筑师
probationer	实习生
process flowchart	工艺流程图
process technology	工艺
project manager (PM)	项目经理
project specification	工程说明
quake-proof	防震
quantity	数量
radiation	辐射
raw material	原材料

reconstruction	改建
rectangle	矩形
reinforced concrete	钢筋混凝土
remarks	备注
rows and columns	行和栏
rural architecture	农村建筑
rust-proof	防锈
segment	弓形
scale	比例尺
schedule of design	设计进度
scheme, draft	方案
section	剖面
sectional dimension	截面尺寸
sector	扇形
semi-open type	半开敞式
serial No.	序列号
service area	辅助面积
side elevation	侧立面
side light	侧光
single span	单跨
site	现场
site area	厂区占地

sketch	草图
solid line	实线
sound absorption	吸音
sound-proof	隔音
spherical	球形的
square	方形
stainless steel	不锈钢
standard drawing	标准图
standardized buildings	标准化建筑
standards and codes	标准规范
steel pipe(tube)	钢管
straight line	直线
sump pit	集水坑
sunshade	遮阳板；遮阳
sunshine	日照
suspended ceiling	吊顶
tables	表格
tangent line	切线
technical and economical index	技术经济指标
technician	技术员
telecommunication	电信
thermal insulation	保温

ton	吨
top light	顶光
topographical map	地形图
traffic volume	车流量
triangle	三角形
typical detail	典型节点
unit cost	单位造价
urban architecture	城市建筑
usable area	使用面积
vapor-proof	隔汽
variable dimension	变尺寸
volume	体积
water supply and drainage	给排水
water-proof	防水
weight	重量
within site	厂区内
working schedule	工程进度表
zigzag line	曲折线

参 考 文 献

[1] 黄荣恩. 科技英语翻译浅说 [M]. 北京：中国对外翻译出版公司，1981.

[2] 武守信，陈伟庆. 科技英语 [M]. 北京：中国铁道出版社，2002.

[3] Kelly Wiles. *Field Guildes to Finding A New Career：Engineering, Mechanics, and Architecture* [M]. USA：Ferguson Press，2009.

[4] B. C. Punmia. *Building Construction* [M]. lands：Laxmi Publications，1993.

[5] P. C. Varghese. *Building Materials* [M]. India：PHI Learning Private Limited，2005.

[6] Zongjin Li. *Advanced Concrete Technology* [M]. USA：John Wiley & Sons, Inc.，2011.

[7] Jan H. Loedeman. *Simple Construction Surveying for Rural Applications* [M]. Netherlands：Agromisa Foundation，2005.

[8] Criss B. Mills. *Designing with Models：A Studio Guide to Architectural Process Models* [M]. USA：John Wiley & Sons, Inc.，2011.

[9] David A. Day, Neal B. H. Benjamin. *Construction Equipment Guide* [M]. USA：John Wiley & Sons, Inc.，2011.

[10] American Institute of Architects. *The architect's handbook of professional practice* [M]. Fourteenth Edition. USA：John Wiley & Sons, Inc.，2008.

[11] http：//books. google. com

[12] http：//civilengineerlink. com

北京大学出版社高职高专土建系列规划教材

序号	书名	书号	编著者	定价	出版时间	印次	配套情况	
基础课程									
1	工程建设法律与制度	978-7-301-14158-8	唐茂华	26.00	2012.7	6	ppt/pdf	
2	建设法规及相关知识	978-7-301-22748-0	唐茂华等	34.00	2013.8	1	ppt/pdf	
3	建设工程法规	978-7-301-16731-1	高玉兰	30.00	2013.8	13	ppt/pdf/答案/素材	★
4	建筑工程法规实务	978-7-301-19321-1	杨陈慧等	43.00	2012.1	4	ppt/pdf	★
5	建筑法规	978-7-301-19371-6	董伟等	39.00	2013.1	4	ppt/pdf	
6	建设工程法规	978-7-301-20912-7	王先恕	32.00	2012.7	2	ppt/pdf	
7	AutoCAD 建筑制图教程(第2版)(新规范)	978-7-301-21095-6	郭慧	38.00	2013.8	2	ppt/pdf/素材	★
8	AutoCAD 建筑绘图教程(2010版)	978-7-301-19234-4	唐英敏等	41.00	2011.7	4	ppt/pdf	
9	建筑CAD项目教程(2010版)	978-7-301-20979-0	郭慧	38.00	2012.9	1	pdf/素材	
10	建筑工程专业英语	978-7-301-15376-5	吴承霞	20.00	2013.8	8	ppt/pdf	
11	建筑工程专业英语	978-7-301-20003-2	韩薇等	24.00	2014.7	2	ppt/pdf	
12	建筑工程应用文写作	978-7-301-18962-7	赵立等	40.00	2012.6	3	ppt/pdf	
13	建筑识图与构造(第2版)(新规范)	978-7-301-14465-7	郑贵超	40.00	2014.1	1	ppt/pdf/答案	★
14	建筑构造(新规范)	978-7-301-21267-7	肖芳	34.00	2013.5	2	ppt/pdf	
15	房屋建筑构造	978-7-301-19883-4	李少红	26.00	2012.1	3	ppt/pdf	
16	建筑工程制图与识图	978-7-301-15443-4	白丽红	25.00	2013.7	9	ppt/pdf/答案	★
17	建筑制图习题集	978-7-301-15404-5	白丽红	25.00	2013.7	8	pdf	
18	建筑制图(第2版)(新规范)	978-7-301-21146-5	高丽荣	32.00	2013.2	1	ppt/pdf	★
19	建筑制图习题集(第2版)(新规范)	978-7-301-21288-2	高丽荣	28.00	2013.1	1	pdf	
20	建筑工程制图(第2版)(附习题册)(新规范)	978-7-301-21120-5	肖明和	48.00	2012.8	5	ppt/pdf	
21	建筑制图与识图	978-7-301-18806-4	曹雪梅等	24.00	2012.2	5	ppt/pdf	★
22	建筑制图与识图习题册	978-7-301-18652-7	曹雪梅等	30.00	2012.4	4	pdf	★
23	建筑制图与识图(新规范)	978-7-301-20070-4	李元玲	28.00	2012.8	4	ppt/pdf	
24	建筑制图与识图习题集(新规范)	978-7-301-20425-2	李元玲	24.00	2012.3	4	ppt/pdf	
25	新编建筑工程制图(新规范)	978-7-301-21140-3	方筱松	30.00	2012.8	1	ppt/pdf	★
26	新编建筑工程制图习题集(新规范)	978-7-301-16834-9	方筱松	22.00	2012.9	1	pdf	
27	建筑识图(新规范)	978-7-301-21893-8	邓志勇等	35.00	2013.1	2	ppt/pdf	
28	建筑识图与房屋构造	978-7-301-22860-9	负禄等	54.00	2013.8	1	ppt/pdf/答案	★
29	建筑构造与设计	978-7-301-23506-5	陈玉萍	38.00	2014.1	1	ppt/pdf/答案	★
30	房屋建筑构造	978-7-301-23588-1	李元玲等	45.00	2014.1	1	ppt/pdf	★
31	建筑制图与识图(第2版)	978-7-301-24386-2	曹雪梅	36.00	2014.9	1	ppt/pdf	
建筑施工类									
1	建筑工程测量	978-7-301-16727-4	赵景利	30.00	2013.8	10	ppt/pdf/答案	★
2	建筑工程测量(第2版)(新规范)	978-7-301-22002-3	张敬伟	37.00	2013.5	2	ppt/pdf/答案	
3	建筑工程测量	978-7-301-19992-3	潘益民	38.00	2012.2	2	ppt/pdf	★
4	建筑工程测量实验与实训指导(第2版)	978-7-301-23166-1	张敬伟	27.00	2013.9	1	pdf/答案	
5	建筑工程测量	978-7-301-13578-5	王金玲等	26.00	2011.8	3	pdf	
6	建筑工程测量实训	978-7-301-19329-7	杨凤华	27.00	2013.5	4	pdf	★
7	建筑工程测量(含实验指导手册)	978-7-301-19364-8	石东等	43.00	2012.6	2	ppt/pdf/答案	★
8	建筑工程测量	978-7-301-22485-4	景铎等	34.00	2013.6	1	ppt/pdf	
9	数字测图技术(新规范)	978-7-301-22656-8	赵红	36.00	2013.6	1	ppt/pdf	★
10	数字测图技术实训指导(新规范)	978-7-301-22679-7	赵红	27.00	2013.6	1	ppt/pdf	★
11	建筑施工技术(新规范)	978-7-301-21209-7	陈雄辉	39.00	2013.2	2	ppt/pdf	★
12	建筑施工技术	978-7-301-12336-2	朱永祥等	38.00	2012.4	7	ppt/pdf	
13	建筑施工技术	978-7-301-16726-7	叶雯等	44.00	2013.5	2	ppt/pdf/素材	
14	建筑施工技术	978-7-301-19499-7	董伟等	42.00	2011.9	1	ppt/pdf	
15	建筑施工技术	978-7-301-19997-8	苏小梅	38.00	2013.5	3	ppt/pdf	
16	建筑工程施工技术(第2版)(新规范)	978-7-301-21093-2	钟汉华等	48.00	2013.8	2	ppt/pdf	★
17	基础工程施工(新规范)	978-7-301-20917-2	董伟等	35.00	2012.7	2	ppt/pdf	★

序号	书名	书号	编著者	定价	出版时间	印次	配套情况	
18	建筑施工技术实训(第2版)	978-7-301-24368-8	周晓龙	30.00	2014.7	1	pdf	★
19	建筑力学(第2版)(新规范)	978-7-301-21695-8	石立安	46.00	2013.9	3	ppt/pdf	★
20	土力学与地基基础	978-7-301-23675-8	叶火炎等	35.00	2014.1	1	ppt/pdf	★
21	土木工程实用力学	978-7-301-15598-1	马景善	30.00	2013.1	4	pdf/ppt	★
22	土木工程力学	978-7-301-16864-6	吴明军	38.00	2011.11	2	ppt/pdf	★
23	PKPM软件的应用(第2版)	978-7-301-22625-4	王 娜等	34.00	2013.6	1	pdf	★
24	建筑结构(第2版)(上册)(新规范)	978-7-301-21106-9	徐锡权	41.00	2013.4	1	ppt/pdf/答案	★
25	建筑结构(第2版)(下册)(新规范)	978-7-301-22584-4	徐锡权	42.00	2013.6	1	ppt/pdf/答案	★
26	建筑结构	978-7-301-19171-2	唐春平等	41.00	2012.6	4	ppt/pdf	
27	建筑结构基础(新规范)	978-7-301-21125-0	王中发	36.00	2012.8	2	ppt/pdf	
28	建筑结构原理及应用	978-7-301-18732-6	史美东	45.00	2012.8	1	ppt/pdf	
29	建筑力学与结构(第2版)(新规范)	978-7-301-22148-8	吴承霞等	49.00	2013.12	2	ppt/pdf/答案	★
30	建筑力学与结构(少学时版)	978-7-301-21730-6	吴承霞	34.00	2013.12	2	ppt/pdf/答案	★
31	建筑力学与结构	978-7-301-20988-2	陈水广	32.00	2012.8	1	pdf/ppt	
32	建筑结构与施工图(新规范)	978-7-301-22188-4	朱希文等	35.00	2013.3	2	ppt/pdf	★
33	生态建筑材料	978-7-301-19588-2	陈剑峰等	38.00	2013.7		ppt/pdf	
34	建筑材料	978-7-301-13576-1	林祖宏	35.00	2012.6	9	ppt/pdf	★
35	建筑材料与检测	978-7-301-16728-1	梅 杨等	26.00	2012.11	8	ppt/pdf/答案	★
36	建筑材料检测试验指导	978-7-301-16729-8	王美芬等	18.00	2013.7	5	pdf	
37	建筑材料与检测	978-7-301-19261-0	王 辉	35.00	2012.6	5	ppt/pdf	★
38	建筑材料与检测试验指导	978-7-301-20045-2	王 辉	20.00	2013.1	3	ppt/pdf	
39	建筑材料选择与应用	978-7-301-21948-5	申淑荣等	39.00	2013.3	1	ppt/pdf	
40	建筑材料检测实训	978-7-301-22317-8	申淑荣等	24.00	2013.4	1	pdf	
41	建设工程监理概论(第2版)(新规范)	978-7-301-20854-0	徐锡权等	43.00	2013.7	3	ppt/pdf/答案	
42	建设工程监理	978-7-301-15017-7	斯 庆	26.00	2013.1	6	ppt/pdf/答案	
43	建设工程监理概论	978-7-301-15518-9	曾庆军等	24.00	2012.12	5	ppt/pdf	
44	工程建设监理案例分析教程	978-7-301-18984-9	刘志麟等	38.00	2013.2	2		★
45	地基与基础(第2版)	978-7-301-23304-7	肖明和等	42.00	2014.1	1	ppt/pdf/答案	★
46	地基与基础	978-7-301-16130-2	孙平平等	26.00	2013.2	3	ppt/pdf	
47	地基与基础实训	978-7-301-23174-6	肖明和等	25.00	2013.10	1		
48	建筑工程质量事故分析(第2版)	978-7-301-22467-0	郑文新	32.00	2013.9	1		★
49	建筑工程施工组织设计	978-7-301-18512-4	李源清	26.00	2013.5	5		★
49	建筑工程施工组织实训	978-7-301-18961-0	李源清	40.00	2012.11	3		★
50	建筑施工组织与进度控制(新规范)	978-7-301-21223-3	张廷瑞	36.00	2012.9	2		★
51	建筑施工组织项目式教程	978-7-301-19901-5	杨红玉	44.00	2012.1	1	ppt/pdf/答案	
52	钢筋混凝土工程施工与组织	978-7-301-19587-1	高 雁	32.00	2012.5	1	ppt/pdf	
53	钢筋混凝土工程施工与组织实训指导(学生工作页)	978-7-301-21208-0	高 雁	20.00	2012.9	1	ppt	
54	建筑力学与结构	978-7-301-23348-1	杨丽君等	44.00	2014.1	1	ppt/pdf	
55	土力学与基础工程	978-7-301-23590-4	宁培淋等	32.00	2014.1	1	ppt/pdf	
工程管理类								
1	建筑工程经济(第2版)	978-7-301-22736-7	张宁宁等	30.00	2013.11	2	ppt/pdf/答案	
2	建筑工程经济	978-7-301-20855-7	赵小娥等	32.00	2013.7	2	ppt/pdf	
3	建筑工程经济	978-7-301-24346-6	刘晓丽等	38.00	2014.7	1	pdf	
4	施工企业会计(第2版)	978-7-301-24434-0	辛艳红等	36.00	2014.7	1	ppt/pdf/答案	★
5	建筑工程项目管理	978-7-301-12335-5	范红岩等	30.00	2012.4	9	ppt/pdf	★
6	建设工程项目管理	978-7-301-16730-4	王 辉	32.00	2013.5	5	ppt/pdf/答案	★
7	建设工程项目管理	978-7-301-19335-8	冯松山等	38.00	2013.11	3	pdf/ppt	
8	建设工程招投标与合同管理(第2版)(新规范)	978-7-301-21002-4	宋春岩	38.00	2013.8	5	ppt/pdf/答案/试题/教案	★
9	建设工程招投标与合同管理(新规范)	978-7-301-16802-8	程超胜	30.00	2012.9	2	ppt/pdf	★
10	建筑工程商务标编制实训	978-7-301-20804-5	钟振宇	35.00	2012.7		ppt	★
11	工程招投标与合同管理实务	978-7-301-19035-7	杨甲奇等	48.00	2011.8	2	pdf	★
12	工程招投标与合同管理实务	978-7-301-19290-0	郑文新等	43.00	2012.4	2	ppt/pdf	★
13	建设工程招投标与合同管理实务	978-7-301-20404-7	杨云会等	42.00	2012.4	1	ppt/pdf/答案/习题库	

序号	书名	书号	编著者	定价	出版时间	印次	配套情况	
14	工程招投标与合同管理(新规范)	978-7-301-17455-5	文新平	37.00	2012.9	1	ppt/pdf	★
15	工程项目招投标与合同管理	978-7-301-15549-3	李洪军等	30.00	2013.11	8	ppt	★
16	工程项目招投标与合同管理(第2版)	978-7-301-22462-5	周艳冬	35.00	2013.7	1	ppt/pdf	★
17	建筑工程安全管理	978-7-301-19455-3	宋 健等	36.00	2013.5	3	ppt/pdf	
18	建筑工程质量与安全管理	978-7-301-16070-1	周连起	35.00	2013.2	5	ppt/pdf/答案	
19	施工项目质量与安全管理	978-7-301-21275-2	钟汉华	45.00	2012.10	1	ppt/pdf	
20	工程造价控制	978-7-301-14466-4	斯 庆	26.00	2013.8	9	ppt/pdf	★
21	工程造价管理	978-7-301-20655-3	徐锡权等	33.00	2013.8	2	ppt/pdf	
22	工程造价控制与管理	978-7-301-19366-2	胡新萍等	30.00	2013.1	1	ppt/pdf	★
23	建筑工程造价管理	978-7-301-20360-6	柴 琦等	27.00	2013.1	1	ppt/pdf	
24	建筑工程造价管理	978-7-301-15517-2	李茂英等	24.00	2012.1	4	pdf	
25	建筑工程造价	978-7-301-21892-1	孙咏梅	40.00	2013.2	1	ppt/pdf	★
26	建筑工程计量与计价(第2版)	978-7-301-22078-8	肖明和等	58.00	2013.8	2	pdf/ppt	★
27	建筑工程计量与计价实训（第2版）	978-7-301-22606-3	肖明和等	29.00	2013.7	1	pdf	★
28	建筑工程计量与计价综合实训	978-7-301-23568-3	龚小兰	28.00	2014.1	1	pdf	★
29	建筑工程估价	978-7-301-22802-9	张 英	43.00	2013.8	1	ppt/pdf	
30	建筑工程计量与计价——透过案例学造价	978-7-301-16071-8	张 强	50.00	2013.9	7	ppt/pdf	
31	安装工程计量与计价（第2版）	978-7-301-22140-2	冯钢等	50.00	2013.7	2	pdf/ppt	
32	安装工程计量与计价实训	978-7-301-19336-5	景巧玲等	36.00	2013.5	3	pdf/素材	
33	建筑水电安装工程计量与计价(新规范)	978-7-301-21198-4	陈连姝	36.00	2013.8	1	ppt/pdf	
34	建筑与装饰装修工程工程量清单	978-7-301-17331-2	翟丽旻等	25.00	2012.8	3	pdf/ppt/答案	
35	建筑工程清单编制	978-7-301-19387-7	叶晓容	24.00	2011.8	2	ppt/pdf	★
36	建设项目评估	978-7-301-20068-1	高志云等	32.00	2013.6	2	ppt/pdf	★
37	钢筋工程清单编制	978-7-301-20114-5	贾莲英	36.00	2012.2	1	ppt / pdf	
38	混凝土工程清单编制	978-7-301-20384-2	顾 娟	28.00	2012.5	1	ppt / pdf	
39	建筑装饰工程预算	978-7-301-20567-9	范菊雨	38.00	2013.6	2	pdf/ppt	★
40	建设工程安全监理(新规范)	978-7-301-20802-1	沈万岳	28.00	2012.7	1	pdf/ppt	★
41	建筑工程安全技术与管理实务(新规范)	978-7-301-21187-8	沈万岳	48.00	2012.9	2	pdf/ppt	★
42	建筑工程资料管理	978-7-301-17456-2	孙 刚等	36.00	2013.8	3	pdf/ppt	
43	建筑施工组织与管理(第2版)(新规范)	978-7-301-22149-5	翟丽旻等	43.00	2013.4	1	ppt/pdf/答案	★
44	建设工程合同管理	978-7-301-22612-4	刘庭江	46.00	2013.6	1	ppt/pdf/答案	
45	工程造价案例分析	978-7-301-22985-9	甄 凤	30.00	2013.8	1	pdf/ppt	★
46	建设工程造价控制与管理	978-7-301-24273-5	胡芳珍等	38.00	2014.6	1	ppt/pdf/答案	★
建筑设计类								
1	中外建筑史	978-7-301-15606-3	袁新华	30.00	2013.8	9	ppt/pdf	★
2	建筑室内空间历程	978-7-301-19338-9	张伟孝	53.00	2011.8	1	pdf	★
3	建筑装饰CAD项目教程(新规范)	978-7-301-20950-9	郭 慧	35.00	2013.1	1	ppt/素材	
4	室内设计基础	978-7-301-15613-1	李书青	32.00	2013.5	3	ppt/pdf	
5	建筑装饰构造	978-7-301-15687-2	赵志文等	27.00	2012.11	5	ppt/pdf/答案	★
6	建筑装饰材料(第2版)	978-7-301-22356-7	焦 涛等	34.00	2013.5	4	ppt/pdf	
7	建筑装饰施工技术	978-7-301-15439-7	王 军等	30.00	2013.7	6	ppt/pdf	★
8	装饰材料与施工	978-7-301-15677-3	宋志春等	30.00	2010.8	1	ppt/pdf/答案	
9	设计构成	978-7-301-15504-2	戴碧锋	30.00	2012.10	1	ppt/pdf	
10	基础色彩	978-7-301-16072-5	张 军	42.00	2011.9	2	pdf	
11	设计色彩	978-7-301-21211-0	龙黎黎	46.00	2012.9	1	ppt	★
12	设计素描	978-7-301-22391-8	司马金桃	29.00	2013.4	1	ppt	★
13	建筑素描表现与创意	978-7-301-15541-7	于修国	25.00	2012.11	3	Pdf	★
14	3ds Max 效果图制作	978-7-301-22870-8	刘 晗等	45.00	2013.7	1	ppt	★
15	3ds Max 室内设计表现方法	978-7-301-17762-4	徐海军	32.00	2010.9	1	pdf	
16	3ds Max 2011室内设计案例教程(第2版)	978-7-301-15693-3	伍福军等	39.00	2011.9	1	ppt/pdf	
17	Photoshop 效果图后期制作	978-7-301-16073-2	脱忠伟等	52.00	2011.1	1	素材/pdf	★
18	建筑表现技法	978-7-301-19216-0	张 峰	32.00	2013.1	2	ppt/pdf	
19	建筑速写	978-7-301-20441-2	张 峰	30.00	2012.4	1	pdf	★
20	建筑装饰设计	978-7-301-20022-3	杨丽君	36.00	2012.2	1	ppt/素材	
21	装饰施工读图与识图	978-7-301-19991-6	杨丽君	33.00	2012.5	1	ppt	

序号	书名	书号	编著者	定价	出版时间	印次	配套情况	
22	建筑装饰工程计量与计价	978-7-301-20055-1	李茂英	42.00	2013.7	2	ppt/pdf	
规 划 园 林 类								
1	居住区景观设计	978-7-301-20587-7	张群成	47.00	2012.5	1	ppt	★
2	居住区规划设计	978-7-301-21031-4	张 燕	48.00	2012.8	2	ppt	★
3	园林植物识别与应用(新规范)	978-7-301-17485-2	潘利等	34.00	2012.9	1	ppt	★
4	城市规划原理与设计	978-7-301-21505-0	谭婧婧等	35.00	2013.1	1	ppt/pdf	★
5	园林工程施工组织管理(新规范)	978-7-301-22364-2	潘利等	35.00	2013.4	1	ppt/pdf	★
房 地 产 类								
1	房地产开发与经营(第2版)	978-7-301-23084-8	张建中等	33.00	2013.8	1	ppt/pdf/答案	★
2	房地产估价(第2版)	978-7-301-22945-3	张 勇等	35.00	2013.8	1	ppt/pdf/答案	★
3	房地产估价理论与实务	978-7-301-19327-3	褚菁晶	35.00	2011.8	1	ppt/pdf/答案	★
4	物业管理理论与实务	978-7-301-19354-9	裴艳慧	52.00	2011.9	1	ppt/pdf	★
5	房地产测绘	978-7-301-22747-3	唐春平	29.00	2013.7	1	ppt/pdf	★
6	房地产营销与策划(新规范)	978-7-301-18731-9	应佐萍	42.00	2012.8	1	ppt/pdf	★
市 政 路 桥 类								
1	市政工程计量与计价(第2版)	978-7-301-20564-8	郭良娟等	42.00	2013.8	3	pdf/ppt	
2	市政工程计价	978-7-301-22117-4	彭以舟等	39.00	2013.2	1	ppt/pdf	★
3	市政桥梁工程	978-7-301-16688-8	刘 江等	42.00	2012.10	2	ppt/pdf/素材	
4	市政工程材料	978-7-301-22452-6	郑晓国	37.00	2013.5	1	ppt/pdf/素材	★
5	路基路面工程	978-7-301-19299-3	偶昌宝等	34.00	2011.8	1	ppt/pdf	
6	道路工程技术	978-7-301-19363-1	刘 雨等	33.00	2011.12	1	ppt/pdf	★
7	城市道路设计与施工(新规范)	978-7-301-21947-8	吴颖峰	39.00	2013.1	1	ppt/pdf	
8	建筑给水排水工程	978-7-301-20047-6	叶巧云	38.00	2012.2	1	ppt/pdf	
9	市政工程测量(含技能训练手册)	978-7-301-20474-0	刘宗波等	41.00	2012.5	1	ppt/pdf	
10	公路工程任务承揽与合同管理	978-7-301-21133-5	邱 兰等	30.00	2012.9	1	ppt/pdf/答案	
11	道桥工程材料	978-7-301-21170-0	刘水林等	43.00	2012.9	1	ppt/pdf	
12	工程地质与土力学(新规范)	978-7-301-20723-9	杨仲元	40.00	2012.6	1	ppt/pdf	★
13	数字测图技术应用教程	978-7-301-20334-7	刘宗波	36.00	2012.8	1	ppt	
14	水泵与水泵站技术	978-7-301-22510-3	刘振华	40.00	2013.5	1	ppt/pdf	★
15	道路工程测量(含技能训练手册)	978-7-301-21967-6	田树涛等	45.00	2013.2	1	ppt/pdf	
建 筑 设 备 类								
1	建筑设备基础知识与识图	978-7-301-16716-8	靳慧征	34.00	2013.11	12	ppt/pdf	★
2	建筑设备识图与施工工艺	978-7-301-19377-8	周业梅	38.00	2011.8	3	ppt/pdf	★
3	建筑施工机械	978-7-301-19365-5	吴志强	30.00	2013.7	3	pdf/ppt	★
4	智能建筑环境设备自动化(新规范)	978-7-301-21090-1	余志强	40.00	2012.8	1	pdf/ppt	★

相关教学资源如电子课件、电子教材、习题答案等可以登录 www.pup6.com 下载或在线阅读。

扑六知识网(www.pup6.com)有海量的相关教学资源和电子教材供阅读及下载(包括北京大学出版社第六事业部的相关资源),同时欢迎您将教学课件、视频、教案、素材、习题、试卷、辅导材料、课改成果、设计作品、论文等教学资源上传到 pup6.com,与全国高校师生分享您的教学成就与经验,并可自由设定价格,知识也能创造财富。具体情况请登录网站查询。

如您需要免费纸质样书用于教学,欢迎登录第六事业部门户网(www.pup6.cn)填表申请,并欢迎在线登记选题以到北京大学出版社来出版您的大作,也可下载相关表格填写后发到我们的邮箱,我们将及时与您取得联系并做好全方位的服务。

扑六知识网将打造成全国最大的教育资源共享平台,欢迎您的加入——让知识有价值,让教学无界限,让学习更轻松。

联系方式:010-62750667,yangxinglu@126.com,linzhangbo@126.com,欢迎来电来信咨询。